Church and Revolution

*Continuing the Conversation between
Christianity and Marxism*

— SIMON HEWITT —

Sacristy
Press

Sacristy Press
PO Box 612, Durham, DH1 9HT

www.sacristy.co.uk

First published in 2020 by Sacristy Press, Durham

Sacristy Limited, registered in England & Wales, number 7565667

British Library Cataloguing-in-Publication Data
A catalogue record for the book is available from the British Library

ISBN 978-1-78959-091-3

For Tasia

Preface

In 2001, I was on a train chartered to take anti-capitalist activists, of whom I was one, from French ferry ports to anti-G8 protests in Genoa, Italy. As it happens, our train had attracted some attention in the press, with columnists solemnly asking whether "those who run riot" ought to be allowed to "run trains".[1] There was speculation about the suspension of the EU's Schengen agreement on freedom of movement, and a good deal of high-level manoeuvring to stop the train running, halted only when the French rail unions made it clear that if this train didn't run, neither would any other train that day. Later these protests would be remembered for the police killing of Carlo Giuliani.[2]

I recall quite vividly ten minutes during that train journey: the train was crowded, the atmosphere somewhere between a party and a meeting. People talked politics; food was shared out. Some tried to sleep; others played games. There was a mix of ages and backgrounds. Amidst the murmur and excitement, the smells of crisps and unwashed armpits, I opened my office book, a book of daily prayers, and read through evening prayer. At the time I felt no tension between radical political practice and Christian faith. Over the subsequent years, I encountered socialists who met my religious practice with either incredulity or hostility and, more often, Christians who denounced my politics. In spite of all this, I remain committed now, as I was then, to both Christianity and Marxism.

Autobiography is not always the best way to begin a book, and obsession with the microscopic details of individual lives is a pathology of the contemporary left. If the personal is political, there is also a politics of knowing when to move beyond the particular and self-focused to the universal and communal. It is never "all about me", no matter who one might be. Yet my suspicion is that there are a significant number of people in the same position as me, somehow clinging to both Christianity and, if not to Marxism, to radical left-wing politics of some kind. One of my purposes in writing this book is to share my own thinking through of the relationship between faith and politics with these people.

Still, neither Christianity nor Marxism are doing well in twenty-first-century Britain. The closest many people come to collective worship is watching football (as cults go, this has a lot to recommend it), and while I was cheered up no end by Jeremy Corbyn's leadership of the Labour Party, his is a socialism of the old Bennite type, ungrounded in any kind of systematic thought. Whatever the more paranoid fantasies of the right-wing press might suggest, the Labour Party has not just finished a period of being led by a Marxist.[3] Nor is it full of Marxists. If it were, I would be considerably more optimistic than I in fact am.

Why, then, inflict this book on the reading public, if neither of the practices[4] it seeks to reconcile have much currency? Why a book on Christianity and Marxism, rather than one on football and dendrochronology, or dog walking and algebra? The beginnings of an answer can be had by looking at the months after the Genoa protest. On 11 September 2001, two planes crashed into the twin towers of the World Trade Center, and that act of mass murder continues to set the political agenda nearly two decades on.

The events of 9/11 put religion back onto the agenda first and foremost through directing a searchlight of suspicion onto Muslims.[5] Most of the left opposed this Islamophobia, but its capacity to do so effectively and in solidarity with Muslims themselves was hampered by a widespread failure to understand religion. The image of religion on the most part held by individual socialists was (and still often is) a caricature, having more in common with the uninformed hostility of Richard Dawkins than the sophisticated criticism of Karl Marx. Islam is not the topic of this book, and I would not be qualified to write on it. Nevertheless, through showing that religion needn't be some kind of rival to science, allied of necessity to reactionary politics, I hope to challenge preconceptions and do something to make possible the kind of conversations between the political left and religious people which need to happen in so many communities.

Since 2001, since the 2007–8 financial crisis and imposition of austerity, and—perhaps most bizarrely of all—since the rise to political prominence of Donald Trump, Christian religiosity has been harnessed by the right in the United States. A multiply married philanderer is not the most obvious poster boy for Christian family values: Marxists will suggest that the contradiction between Trump's actions and the professed values of his religious base show that the motivations of the latter are, at root, other than religious. Trump's evangelical cheerleaders themselves are more likely to insist that God moves in mysterious ways: who knows if Trump is not one of those ways? Either way, the Christian right is a major political actor in the US.

This is not the case in Britain.[6] Conservative politicians, in an attempt to sustain an ideology of national unity first in the face of their imposition of austerity, then of the deep divisions around Brexit, have made appeal to "Christian values" and "Christian heritage". But it is not a serious religiosity which is being invoked. Christianity functions in this way of thinking as a backdrop to a nostalgic picture of a Britain once great. This is the kind of Christianity which sighs contentedly while listening to *Carols from King's* and eating mince pies, not the kind that studies the letters of Saint Paul.

What religious right there is in Britain is marginal, taking the form either of bizarre outfits such as Christian

Voice[7] or else particular mobilizations around "family" and bioethical issues. Whilst left-wing Christians might worry, at least about the latter, as a funnel for their co-religionists into right-wing politics, the impact of these currents on public life in Britain is slight. In fact, the only case of right-wing Christianity having a recent impact on British parliamentary politics is from across the Irish Sea, through the role of the Democratic Unionist Party (DUP) in shoring up the Conservative government after the 2017 general election.

Discounting the DUP, the Christian right is no threat to people in Britain, although people who happen to be both right-wing and Christian certainly are. In spite of this, my experience is of an increasing felt need on the part of British left-wing activists to attack an imagined religious right. There seems to be a generational shift at work here, and the immediacy of contact with US debates made possible by the internet, and especially by social media, has been a big factor. The culture-wars framing of these US debates has also been imported unthinkingly, with domestic strife over EU membership providing the cover. If to be left-wing is to be the kind of person who reads *The Guardian* in a hipster coffee bar, rather than the kind of person who reads a gardening magazine at a carvery, to be left-wing is surely to be without religion (however "spiritual" one might profess oneself to be). This picture is a travesty, and the implications for left-wing politics of casually excluding millions of religious people from its remit potentially disastrous. In laying out how I think about the relationship between Marxism and Christianity, one aim is to show secular leftists how religion needn't force a reactionary political stance. Another is to suggest to my fellow Christians that they needn't follow a conservative path in reconciling their faith to politics.

This book is about something called "Christianity" and something called "Marxism". But one is never just a Marxist or just a Christian (C. S. Lewis' book *Mere Christianity* did a lot of damage in convincing people otherwise with respect to the latter). Each tradition contains sub-traditions of its own, immersion in which affects how one understands the parent tradition. Some years back, in an enduringly readable book on Christianity and Marxism, Andrew Collier made a backhanded jibe at the Christian–Marxist dialogues of the 1960s, saying that it is easy to reconcile "humanist Marxism with Pelagian Christianity".[8] I imagine that Collier, an undervalued thinker whose early death was a loss to the British left, would have thought that the present book is a case in point. I am certainly not a Pelagian,[9] but I do stand in a Roman Catholic, specifically Dominican, tradition which takes a more optimistic view of human nature than those Christian traditions which shout loudest in contemporary anglophone society. My reading of Marx emphasizes his early "humanistic" works, and stresses their continuity with his later works: other than that, I stand in a broadly Trotskyist tradition, firmly opposed to the kind of degraded Marxism which was found in the former Eastern Bloc. Readers should bear these commitments in mind in assessing what follows.

I am an academic, it being just about possible to earn one's living doing this, in spite of the best efforts of successive governments and a tenacious layer of neo-liberal managers to rid universities of any activities not of immediate benefit to what they term the "business community".[10] This book, however, is not (as critics will no doubt point out) a work of academic philosophy or theology. It draws on these disciplines, with uneven depth, but its point is simply to communicate my thinking about an area I consider important and to stimulate others to think about Marxism and Christianity. In the latter cause, I have referenced Marx's works via the freely available *Marxists Internet Archive*. The footnotes, which are more extensive and lengthier than would be expected in a pamphlet of this size, provide further commentary and references to additional literature to enable readers to pursue topics in greater depth than is possible here.

Even a book as short as this is really a collective endeavour (perhaps this is especially the case with a short book). I have benefitted enormously over the years from talking about Marxism, Christianity, Marxism and Christianity, and religion more generally with Jon Anderson, Graham Bash, Paul Butler, Michael Calderbank, Koshka Duff, Lorna Finlayson, Marcus Flavin, Ian Ilet, Michael Kirwan, Catherine Lafferty, Sam Lebens, Rachel Muers, Livs Nelis, Danielle Sands,

Anastasia Scrutton, Carrie Thompson, Catherine Wallis-Hughes and Bob Wright. None of these will agree with all of what I say. Many of them will disagree with a lot of it; still I am thankful.

Jonathan Nassim read the manuscript and provided a wealth of thoughtful comments and suggestions, many of which, such are the prerogatives of friendship, I have ignored. Another debt is harder to discharge in writing; Marx and Engels wrote that under communism, "the beasts too would be free". Until our dog Lola came on the scene, I was inclined to write this off as mere sentimentality, so she has deepened my understanding, as well as being an amazing companion during the writing of what follows.

Above all else, my thanks go to Tasia, for intellectual insight, political solidarity and love. As good a reason as any for me to continue to adhere to both of the movements which are the subject of this book is that we live in a world in which the chances of love are fleeting and fragile. I am grateful for having been shown why the fight against such a world is worthwhile.

Contents

CHAPTER 1

Atheism

Marx was an atheist and an opponent of organized religion. Over and above this, he viewed his criticisms of religion as somehow integral to his understanding of human society and the possibilities for transforming it. "The criticism of religion is the basis of all criticism", he wrote (adding that as far as the Germany of his day was concerned the task of criticizing religion was complete).[11] So, against those who would effect too easy a reconciliation between Marxism and Christianity, Marx is in agreement with those conservative Christians who regard with suspicion attempts to appeal to Marx as a social theorist without taking on board his critique of religious worldviews.[12]

In this chapter I want to suggest that, while easy reconciliation is ruled out, there remains a way in which Marx's thinking about religion can sit alongside Christian faith. And I want to claim that, quite apart from the benefits of being able to avail ourselves of Marx's thought about society, Christians ought to embrace Marx's critique of belief in God for thoroughly traditional reasons. In brief, anything susceptible to Marx's attack cannot be that which Christians describe in one of our creeds as the "creator of all things, visible and invisible".

Marx against the question of God

Religion is both a practical and a cognitive phenomenon—it involves both practices and beliefs. Marx acknowledges each of these aspects, and religious practice features significantly in his account of human societies. It is, however, religious *belief*, and more generally religious worldviews—ways of seeing the world through the lens of belief in God, an afterlife, and so on—to which he devotes most attention.[13] In one of the best-known and least-understood passages in his work, Marx writes:

> The foundation of irreligious criticism is: *Man makes religion*, religion does not make man. Religion is, indeed, the self-consciousness and self-esteem of man who has either not yet won through to himself, or has already lost himself again. But *man* is no abstract being squatting outside the world. Man is *the world of man*—state, society. This state and this society produce religion, which is an *inverted consciousness of the world*, because they are an *inverted world*.

> Religion is the general theory of this world, its encyclopaedic compendium, its logic in popular form, its spiritual *point d'honneur*, its enthusiasm, its moral sanction, its solemn complement, and its universal basis of consolation and justification. It is the *fantastic realization* of the human essence since the *human essence* has not acquired any true reality. The struggle against religion is, therefore, indirectly the struggle *against that world* whose spiritual *aroma* is religion.
>
> *Religious* suffering is, at one and the same time, the *expression* of real suffering and a *protest* against real suffering. Religion is the sigh of the oppressed creature, the heart of a heartless world, and the soul of soulless conditions. It is the *opium* of the people.[14]

Much ink has been spilled on the interpretation of these two paragraphs, a good deal of the discussion centring on the final declaration that religion is "the opium of the people". The metaphor undoubtedly conveys an ambivalence towards religion. Opium both dulls pain and masks the source of the pain. It comforts and yet entices into addiction. Similarly, thinks Marx, a religious view of the world affords comfort and permits people to go on living in an exploitative society only at the price of distorting their capacity to understand that society. It is an inverted consciousness of the world: the worker thanks God for her daily bread, which in fact is the product of human labour, while the God she thanks (thinks

Marx) is the product of human invention. Things are seen in a topsy-turvy fashion: what is genuinely human is attributed to God, whereas the realities postulated by religious belief are not recognized as human artefacts. And this, according to Marx, is because the world itself is "inverted". What does this mean?

The basic building blocks of Marx's understanding of religion come from the German materialist philosopher Ludwig Feuerbach (1804–72). In his *Essence of Christianity*, Feuerbach had argued that in religious concepts such as *God* and *heaven*, human beings invest the unrealized potentials of their own nature and do so to their own detriment.[15] I may be weak, but God is strong. The world may be terrible, but heaven lies ahead. In this Marx agrees with Feuerbach, religion is "the self-consciousness and self-esteem of man", unrecognized as such by alienated human beings. Where Marx goes beyond Feuerbach is in enquiring into the *origins* of religious alienation. He argues that the imaginary fulfilment of human beings in religion arises out of their unfulfilment in reality. And to understand this, thinks Marx, we need to shift our attention from religion to the underlying causes of religious illusion, to turn "the criticism of heaven into the criticism of earth".

The underlying alienation which finds its illusory healing in religion is, on Marx's view, economic (in the broad sense encompassing humanity's productive and creative activities, and systematic interaction with the non-human world). Wage-labourers under capitalism are unable to fulfil their distinctively human creative nature, lacking control over their own productive activity, and existing in a state of alienation from both each other and non-human nature.[16] Those who employ them (the bourgeoisie) are, whilst better situated materially, also alienated, living in relationships of perpetual competition with one another and exploitative inequality with workers.[17] It is this set-up which gives rise to religious consciousness under capitalism, insists Marx, as did class societies existing before capitalism. Religion will only be done away with by doing away with class society, and it is this task, rather than the denunciation of religion, which ought to occupy revolutionaries.[18]

There is no doubt in the light of this that Marx would have little time for the likes of Richard Dawkins or the other New Atheists. Their criticism of religion as a set of abstract ideas, to be assessed as true or false by disinterested reason apart from social context, makes it a target for the self-same objections Marx raised against Feuerbach.[19] Rather than being a combatant in the debate between theists and atheists, Marx should be understood as a *therapeutic philosopher*. Instead of answering a philosophical question (whether mind and body are two separate substances, for example, or how words come to have meaning) this sort of philosopher makes us aware of the situation out of which the question arises and thereby points us towards a cure of the need to ask it. "The philosopher treats problems", wrote

Wittgenstein, "like an illness".[20] Wittgenstein himself seems to have thought that the question whether God exists stood in need of therapy, although he was much more sympathetic to religion itself than was Marx.[21] That the philosophy of religion needs therapy Marx agrees; it is just that the therapy it requires is drastic indeed: the revolutionary overthrow of the form of society which gives rise to it. Only an unalienated humanity will be free from the temptation to misrepresent its own nature as a deity apart from itself. And only such a humanity will be free from the debate over whether such a deity exists. It is a pleasing implication of the Marxian understanding of socialism that the interventions of A. C. Grayling will be superfluous to requirement.

Opposing the opposition

So much for the basics of Marx's criticism of religion, and so far we might seem to have encountered little of use to the Christian Marxist. Note though that Marx's criticism only gets purchase to the extent that religious concepts *are* merely projections on the part of alienated humanity, signifying nothing beyond themselves. Marx simply assumes that this is the case.[22] No theist is going to agree with him, although the perceptive will recognize the human tendency to build into heaven what we lack on earth, and taking Marx on board will freely acknowledge that social transformation would help us be free from idolatrous conceptions of God. It is in the idea of *idolatry*, frequently linked in scripture to oppression, that I think the best prospect lies for building a bridge between Marx and a Christian understanding of God.

To see this, we need to pay attention to an often-neglected theme in Marx's early writings. Recall that the very persistence of the very question whether God exists is, for Marx, a sign of a society beset with alienation. More especially, he thinks that non-revolutionary atheists are stuck in a symbiosis with religious believers. They only find themselves able to affirm humanity to the extent that they deny God, just as the believer exalts God only through denigrating humanity. The two are stuck in one and the same problematic. The atheist is therefore somehow parasitic upon religion, and both alike face the *Feuerbachian dilemma*: you are for humankind only to the extent that you deny of God what you would have for humankind.[23] Marx thinks that in doing away with the society which gives rise to the dilemma, socialism will abolish atheism:

> But since for the socialist man the *entire so-called history of the world* is nothing but the creation of man through human labour, nothing but the emergence of nature for man, so he has the visible, irrefutable proof of his *birth* through himself, of his *genesis*. Since the *real existence* of man and nature has become evident in practice, through sense experience, because man

> has thus become evident for man as the being of
> nature, and nature for man as the being of man, the
> question about an *alien* being, about a being above
> nature and man—a question which implies the
> admission of the unreality of nature and of man—
> has become impossible in practice. *Atheism* as the
> denial of this unreality, has no longer any meaning,
> for atheism is a *negation of God,* and postulates *the
> existence of man* through this negation; but socialism
> as socialism no longer stands in any need of such a
> mediation.[24]

Theologian Denys Turner has, in several places, made a powerful case that Christian believers ought to join Marx in rejecting any conception of God which functions to diminish human beings, for example by investing God with agency at the expense of human beings. What is particularly arresting in the light of mainstream debates is that Turner, speaking for a long tradition of Christian thought,[25] thinks that not only can the Christian who has joined Marx in his atheistic denials still say "God exists", but further that *only* such a Christian is recognizing with clear sight the implications of belief in God. Says Turner:

> The Marxian critique is, in my view, a criticism of
> a kind of idolatrous religion which is bound always
> to create ideological distortions even within the
> authentic socialist movements whenever, rarely,
> it seeks alliances there. It is not my point that a

non-idolatrous Christianity need expect no trouble from Marx. It is, rather, that, without a radical reintegration of the Marxian critique into the theological and practical project of Christianity, we are unlikely ever to expunge from it the corroding effects of Feuerbach and so of his idolatrous God. To know God we must do justice to Marx.[26]

There is no god in the world

Whatever else we may say of God, God is the creator. This does not mean, as the misleadingly named creationism has it, that God is an alternative explanation for how the world is, competing with and displacing scientific theories. Creationism is a substitute for cosmology and evolutionary theory for the scientifically illiterate or fundamentalist. The doctrine of creation, meanwhile, claims that after science has explained everything in its domain of enquiry there will remain a question, "why is there something, rather than nothing at all?" The word "God" is used for whatever it is that answers this question. We cannot, thinks the strand of Christian thought I'm commending here, say what God is (as, for instance, you can say that I am a mammalian biped, or that water molecules consist of two hydrogen atoms and an oxygen atom bonded in a certain way).[27] On pain of circularity God cannot be one of the things after whose existence we are asking, and our language—developed for talking about such things—is ill-equipped for talking about God. In spite of the tendency of many religious people in their brash over-confidence to give the impression of knowing God's bank details, there is a clear sense in which the classical theism of Augustine or Aquinas is a muted affair. We cannot (in this life) know what God is.

Herbert McCabe sets all of this out nicely:

> To say that we have a valid question (one with an answer) is to say that God exists; for what we mean by "God" is just whatever answers the question. Apart from knowing this, says Aquinas most insistently, all we can do is point, as systematically as we can, to several kinds or categories of things that the answer *could not be*. For one thing, whatever would answer our question could not itself be subject to the question—otherwise we are left as we were, with the same question still to answer. Whatever we mean by "God" cannot be whatever it is that makes us ask the question in the first place. So perishability, decline, dependence, alteration, the impersonality that characterizes material things, and so on—all these have to be excluded from God.[28]

What does this have to do with Marx and the Feuerbachian dilemma? Well, while we cannot comprehend God's nature, the fact that God is whatever answers the "why anything?" question means that we are in a position to say many things about what God is not, as McCabe indicates. And in the process of saying what God is not—known as *apophasis* or negative theology—we come to realize God is not a material object, and does not occupy space or time. God does not have parts (or else the coming together of the parts would stand in need of explanation—whatever the doctrine of the Trinity claims, it cannot consistently be that there are three *parts* of God). God does not possess properties that are distinct from God (for the same reason): the colour of my hair is distinct from me. It is no part of me that I have the particular hair colour I have (indeed, I might easily not have it: one glass of whisky too many and a readily available bottle of hair dye is all it takes); God's wisdom, thinks Aquinas, just is God. Finally, while I might very easily not have existed, and will one day cease to exist, this is not true of God: nothing contingent could be the creator. God is not, we might say, a *thing* amongst other things. It is part of classical Christian theology that there is no such *thing* as God. To suppose otherwise is idolatry, to think of something less than God as God.

Here's how this matters for thinking about Marx. God does not compete for metaphysical space with the things in the world. If I am to exert agency, there will often be a sense in which it is at the expense of some other thing: I cannot drive the car at the same time as you (dual controls excepted). More monumentally, if I liberate you, there is a clear sense in which you do not liberate yourself (compare the benevolent, but paternalistic white opponent of the slave trade with the slave who lays down her tools autonomously). Humankind has often thought about its deities as things in the world, so that they too compete for agency. Think about the Greek and Roman gods, who negotiated with human beings, interacted with them, and could be outwitted or pre-empted by them. That God is the creator entails that God is not such a god. There are no gods in the world.

In the terms I have just used, only a god can get the Feuerbachian dilemma going. Zeus is mighty to the extent that I am weak. But God is not a god. God's agency doesn't crowd me out. God as creator lies behind and is present in human actions. When I do something, God is intimately present in the act as its creator. It doesn't follow that my act is not free, indeed it is because of God that it is free (were God not to create there would be no act, and indeed no me).[29] If Christian faith takes the traditional form of belief in the creator God, then it is at least free of indictment on the grounds of being caught up in the Feuerbachian dilemma and the product of alienation. It can, moreover, enthusiastically agree with Marx that the society which causes this alienation ought to be transcended,[30] not least because this will do away with an impetus to idolatry.

Idolatry and oppression

This is all well and good, but—as atheist polemicists have not been slow to point out in response to accounts of Christian belief like that in the previous section—it seems a long way from what many Christians believe. Surely for many believers God is a person, much like me but more powerful, who "intervenes" from outside situations[31] and can be persuaded to look more kindly on us by a bit of ear-bending (it is usually conceded that the ears, at least, are metaphorical). Whether or not our contemporaries accept God or reject him as a fairy story, it is an anthropomorphic deity they have in mind.

Marx's account of religious illusion predicts that this is precisely how things would be in a society awash with alienation. People will live out their unfulfilled potentials in a world of religious make-believe, or else they will attempt to affirm themselves through rejecting that make-believe (and in so doing make their self-affirmation parasitic upon a fantasy—the prolonged adolescence of many prominent secularist commentators provides a case in point). The Christian tradition I have been describing joins the atheists in rejecting the gods of alienated illusion (many of whom are mistaken for God), while joining with Marx in insisting that we need to oppose the very opposition between God and humanity. It is just that classical Christian theism believes that this can be done in theistic terms, through affirmation of God who is not a god, who is not simply an immensely powerful thing.

My claim is not therefore that Christian belief is not very often caught up in the Feuerbachian dilemma; it very palpably is. The dimly audible good news is that Christians both needn't and oughtn't believe in a way that is susceptible to Marx's critique. That we so frequently do believe in such a way is testimony to the fact that under capitalism, as for the Hebrew Bible,[32] idolatry and domination go hand in hand. In the little that remains of this chapter I want to explore the connection between the two.

McCabe sees the creation faith of the Hebrew Bible as opening the way for a critical understanding of human society:

> [I]t is the God of the Hebrews (who in the Jewish interpretation comes to be seen as creator) who is hailed in the decalogue as liberator; it is the gods (parts of history) and the whole religion of the gods that is seen to stand for alienation and dependency. 'I am the Lord[33] your God who brought you out of slavery; you shall have no gods.'
>
> God the creator, who is not one of the participants in history but the mover of Cyrus and of all history, is the liberator fundamentally because he is not a god, because there are no gods, or at least no gods to be worshipped. This leaves history in human hands under the judgement of God. Human misery can no longer be attributed to the gods and accepted with resignation or evaded with sacrifices. The long slow

> process can begin of identifying the human roots of
> oppression and exploitation, just as the way now lies
> open for the scientific understanding and control of
> the forces of nature.[34]

God's agency does not compete with that of the entities postulated by natural science, since God is not an inhabitant of the universe. By way of exact parallel, God's agency does not compete with that of those realities described by social science and critical theory (the temptation to think otherwise comes from, rightly, observing that these describe free human actions and making the fallacious inference that for a human action to be free is for it to be uncreated).[35] Because of this we can attempt to understand the social world in a non-theological fashion, alongside others of all faiths and none, and use the understanding we gain to transform the world for the better. We do not have the excuse of saying that extreme inequalities of wealth are "God's will" or that climate change is a mere "test of faith". We can develop this-worldly accounts of these things and use those to change them.

One of these non-theological this-worldly accounts is Marxism. And if Marxism's claims are correct, then we can use it to guide our struggle to transform the society which produces the idolatrous belief that to accept Marxism is to deny God's prerogatives. The wheel has come full circle.

CHAPTER 2

Materialism

Marx was a materialist, not in the everyday sense of being grasping (if that were the case, he would have been a very bad materialist, spending much of his life in extreme poverty), but in that of holding a worldview which privileges the material. Subsequent Marxists have followed him in this. For many people (whether Christians, or Marxists, or neither), this fact alone is sufficient to rule out any reconciliation between Marxism and Christianity. For if Marxism entails materialism, so goes the reasoning, then, since materialism is incompatible with Christianity, Marxism too is incompatible with Christianity. That materialism entails atheism might be thought implicit in a well-known moving passage from Trotsky's *Testament*:

> For forty-three years of my conscious life I have
> remained a revolutionist; for forty-two of them I
> have fought under the banner of Marxism. If I had
> to begin all over again, I would of course try and

avoid this or that mistake, but the main course of my life would remain unchanged. I shall die a proletarian revolutionist, *a Marxist, a dialectical materialist, and, consequently, an irreconcilable atheist*. My faith in the communist future of mankind is not less ardent, indeed it is firmer today, than it was in the days of my youth.

Natasha [Trotsky's wife] has just come up to the window from the courtyard and opened it wider so that the air may enter more freely into my room. I can see the bright green strip of grass beneath the wall, and the clear blue sky above the wall, and sunlight everywhere. Life is beautiful. Let the future generations cleanse it of all evil, oppression, and violence and enjoy it to the full.[36]

"A Marxist, a dialectical materialist, and, consequently, an irreconcilable atheist"—dialectical materialism here is a particular understanding of Marxist materialism, mediated by Engels. But it is surely the materialism, rather than the dialectic, which is supposed to come packaged with atheism. Is Trotsky right about this?

If Marxist materialism were a materialism of the kind commonly professed in contemporary philosophy, it certainly would have to entail atheism. Someone who signs up to materialism of this kind holds that everything that exists is a material entity. Since God— if God exists—is not a material entity, materialism of this sort has to include atheism (at best, some sort of pantheism might be salvageable, but that is still atheism concerning God as understood by Christianity).[37]

However, it is not the least bit credible that it was materialism as a *metaphysical* doctrine—a philosophical doctrine concerning the nature of reality as a whole—which Marx advocated. The reason is quite simple: Marx was implacably opposed to metaphysical speculation. The ahistorical contemplative attitude towards the world which he understood metaphysics to require was the polar opposite of the engaged rationality required of revolutionary intellectuals. If there is little in his work by way of sustained dismissal of metaphysics as such (rather than particular metaphysical doctrines, of which more below), that is only because Marx is profoundly uninterested in it, to the extent of not even wanting to channel much of his prodigious energy towards undermining it. Metaphysics makes general claims about reality. The claim that everything is material is a paradigm case. And Marx refuses to make it, consistently with his general refusal of metaphysics.[38]

Whether Marx was correct about metaphysics might be doubted; the British idealist philosopher F. H. Bradley was later to remark that in the act of trying to escape metaphysics, philosophers invariably committed themselves to a metaphysics of their own.[39] Still, that everything is material would be a particularly unfortunate claim for Marx to make. His own work is full of talk of dubiously material entities, what he calls the "real abstractions" arising out of our social life: value, money, the state.[40] Contemporary social philosophers might argue that these are not a great problem for (metaphysical) materialism, since they exist because of material things, namely human beings (as the philosophers in question would prefer to put the point, they are *grounded* in the material world).[41] I think it unlikely that this is right—the issues are complex and relate to the question of reductionism about social reality—but it doesn't really matter for our purposes. There is another, more straightforward challenge to the suggestion that Marxist materialism is metaphysical materialism.

There are, you might think, numbers. For example, there is a number between four and six, namely five. Those philosophers and mathematicians who take this talk at face value are known as *platonists*. Platonists think that numbers exist and that we are not in any sense crossing our fingers when we say that numbers exist. It would take us too far off-topic to explore the reasons that might be offered for or against platonism.[42] But now consider the question; could a platonist about mathematics be a Marxist? The question ought to strike you as bizarre; of course she could, why on earth would someone think otherwise? What someone thinks about mathematical reality is utterly irrelevant to their signing up to Marxism, which is the theory and practice of understanding, in order to abolish by working-class self-emancipation, class society, its structure, ideology and development. And if that is right, the materialism contained within Marxism cannot be metaphysical materialism.

What, then, is Marxist materialism? A decent answer to that question will, assuming there is any such coherent doctrine as Marxist materialism, not rule out positions upon which Marxism ought not to pronounce, and yet will still make a sufficient claim about the world to be interesting and, more importantly for Marx, politically relevant: "Philosophers have only hitherto interpreted the world in various ways, the point is to change it."[43]

Materialism and history

Changing the world is a fraught matter, as anyone who has ever tried to do it will attest. Structures and situations are resistant to our efforts at transformation. Revolutionary organizations limit, as well as facilitate, radical change. The situations in which they find themselves, in any case, dictate what that change could look like. And the needs, health, and available time of their members will determine the extent to which even that is possible. Here, as elsewhere, appeals to dream the impossible and assurances that we can be anything we want to be are invitations to delusion. As Marx wrote:

> People make their own history, but they do not make it as they please; they do not make it under self-selected

> circumstances, but under circumstances existing
> already, given and transmitted from the past.[44]

The commanding obligation of Marxist materialism is to both emphasize and flesh out the phrase "they do not make it under self-selected circumstances". Marx, committed to a socialist future, brought about by the conscious agency of the working class, nonetheless realizes that it is only in a narrow range of circumstances that the birth of this future could take place. His materialism is a view about the nature of history and society, founded on the realization that human beings are material animals, existing in communities and needing to interact with the material world in order to survive. At this point one might wonder who on earth would question this. We'll come onto that; first we should attend to the nature of Marx's view of society.

Marx's account of human societies and the manner in which they change is known as *historical materialism*. Much has been written about this, and there is only space to lay out the essentials here. These begin with Marx's clear observation of the facts that human animals are situated in, and interact with, a material world and that any non-mystificatory explanation[45] of social phenomena must proceed on this basis. It is through acting upon the world, producing food, shelter, and the other things we need in life, that we persist as a species, and so it is a constraint upon the course history takes that we continue to be able to produce. Whatever happens at a given point in human history, if it is not to mark the end of the human story, it cannot involve an end to our capacity to produce enough to satisfy our needs.[46] And what happens must either be consistent with the way production is organized and controlled socially, or else involve radical change in that organization and control (what is called, in the Marxist tradition, *social revolution*).

At any given time the productive set-up of a human society, what Marx calls the *mode of production*, consists of two elements.[47] The *forces of production* are those people, technologies, networks, skills, collections of knowledge, and ways of relating to one another at the level of work which make possible the production of products to satisfy our needs from non-human nature. As history advances, the forces of production develop: once there were neither combine harvesters nor the internet. The *relations of production* meanwhile are those society-wide relations of ownership and control over the means of production (roughly those forces of production other than human beings)[48] and relationships between human beings directly consequent upon these (employment, feudal lordship, and so on). From prehistory to the present day these relations of production have taken the form of class-relations, relations between groups of human beings with distinct interests based on their control of economic activity. Under capitalism the tendency is for the number of classes to reduce down to two: the working class, or proletariat, who sell their power to perform labour to employers for a wage, and the bourgeoisie, those who own a significant amount of the means of production and do not need to work.[49]

There are, thinks Marx, important relationships between these realities. The forces of production are primary, in the sense that anything else which happens in human society has to be compatible with their persistence. In particular, the forces of production constrain the relations of production (Marx sometimes implies more, that they *determine* those relations in a strong sense, but I don't need to claim anything as strong as this here); the two-class set-up of capitalism requires a mass labour force and concentrated production made possible by industrial technology. On the other hand, the forces of production can reach a particular stage of development in which the class organization of society is a "fetter" on their further development.[50] At this point the time is ripe for revolutionary change.

Beyond the inter-relations within a particular mode of production, Marx thinks that the mode of production (called in the present context the *base*, or economic *structure*) conditions the rest of human life, and in particular the cultural, political and intellectual features of society (the *superstructure*). The extent to which we can write books (and what we consider worth writing about), the available materials for education, the amount of time we have to think, and whether a group of people can be spared in order to do this: all of this depends on a basic fact, that we are frail animal beings, who must first ensure our survival before we can do anything else. Someone can only write *War and Peace* if their society can provide them with food without their needing to bring in the harvest themselves. Moreover, the ideas and practices of a society must, for the most part, most of the time, function to support, or at least be compatible with, the persistence of its mode of production. This, which is what Marxists have in mind when they talk about *ideology*, is not a form of conspiracy theory. Marx and Engels' claim that "the ideas of the ruling class are in every epoch the ruling ideas" is prone to be heard otherwise by contemporary ears, but conscious conspiracy is quite foreign to Marx's general understanding of society.[51] The basic Marxian point is that material (economic, social) factors determine, or to use terms less prone to mislead, constrain and condition, our ideas about society and the practices within which those thoughts find embodiment.

Human beings are not creatures of pure intellect, conjuring up ideas outside of any material context. We are animals, situated in material circumstances, which both enable and constrain our thought. Understand that and you have understood the fundamentals of Marx's materialism. As Marx and Engels themselves put it, "[l]ife is not determined by consciousness, but consciousness by life."[52] Now this is not a universal metaphysical claim; rather it is an observation about human beings and our place in the world as thinking beings. It *could* come into conflict with religious belief—imagine a group who, like Plato, believed that knowledge was the result of our disembodied souls having encountered immaterial Forms before our birth, and that this was re-awakened in us during our earthly lives.[53] But Marx's bare materialism needn't come into conflict with religious belief, and in particular there is no reason to think it is incompatible with Christian belief. That is not to say that there are no challenges to Christianity from Marx's thought about society and history. We'll see below that there are some difficulties for church life and doctrine contained in that thought. Before addressing that, though, it will be instructive to consider the philosophical outlook that was Marx's target in his exposition of materialism.[54]

Materialism and idealism

Like the word "materialism" there is an everyday sense to "idealism", suggesting someone's clinging naively, and in the face of the evidence, to some worthwhile but impractical set of ideals. Marx was not and, in spite of a popular image, neither are at least some of his political heirs, idealist in this sense. His political writings exhibit a calculating pragmatism, and it is at least arguable that those present day anti-Marxists who believe that market mechanisms are capable of both providing for the whole human race and safeguarding the natural environment, are more prone to the charge of idealism in this sense than someone clear-sighted enough to recognize the limits of capitalism.

Marx was opposed to idealism in this sense, the preserve of dreamers and hippies (there's a close relationship between it and what he termed "utopianism"). His materialism, however, is directed against idealism in a distinctive philosophical sense of that word. The philosophical idealist believes that all reality is, at root, mental. Berkeley, the great Irish philosopher of the eighteenth century, was a philosophical idealist, holding that to exist is to be perceived, and that therefore the ordinary objects of our everyday experience depend for their existence on our mental activity.[55] To the worry that this would mean that these objects disappear when nobody is around to perceive them (what happens to the laptop I am typing this on when I leave the room to make a coffee?) Berkeley responds that God's perceiving ensures their continuity. The suggestion that God is a perceiver, a being with mental states, implies a very different view of God from the one I appealed to in the previous chapter.

Marx was certainly hostile to idealism of this general philosophical sort, but his particular concern was with idealism concerning human history and society. This latter kind of idealism found its grandest expression in the writings of the philosopher from whom Marx learned most, Hegel. In his *Phenomenology of Spirit*, Hegel presents history as the progress of *Geist*, meaning "spirit" or "mind", gradually coming to self-consciousness, and thereby freedom.[56] As this precis might suggest, the book and its ideas are not the easiest to engage with in the philosophical canon, and while an understanding of them is desirable for getting a proper understanding of Marx they are, thankfully, not required to follow the argument of this chapter.[57] The basic point to take on board is that Marx is opposed to the view that the motor of history consists of ideas. This view he found on a grand metaphysical scale in Hegel's work, but also in those followers of Hegel to whom Marx had himself once been aligned, known as the *left Hegelians.* These differed from Hegel on the question whether the historical progress of Geist had been completed (whether, as they put it, the real was rational), but they were idealists for all that. So, confusingly, in the relevant sense, were materialists such as Feuerbach, who thought that the solution to religious illusion was to instil in people a correct understanding of how religious belief came about. The problem with the world, on this view, is bad ideas. The solution is better ideas.

This gets to the heart of what Marx, the revolutionary, thinks is wrong with idealism. It prevents us understanding how social change comes about. Rather than collective human action on the picket line or at the polling station, aimed ultimately at replacing the existing relations of production, idealism makes social change first and foremost a matter of education. Marx and Engels satirize the view to great effect in *The German Ideology*:

> Once upon a time a valiant fellow had the idea that
> men were drowned in water only because they were
> possessed with the idea of gravity. If they were to
> knock this notion out of their heads, say by stating it
> to be a superstition, a religious concept, they would
> be sublimely proof against any danger from water.
> His whole life long he fought against the illusion of
> gravity, of whose harmful results all statistics brought
> him new and manifold evidence. This valiant fellow
> was the type of the new revolutionary philosophers
> in Germany.[58]

Marx does not deny, of course, that ideas are of political importance. He would hardly have put so much effort into communicating political thought if he doubted this. The subsequent Marxist tradition has built on his work concerning the importance of human understanding of reality, with the contribution of Italian Marxist Antonio Gramsci and the writings of Frankfurt School authors such as Adorno, Horkheimer and Marcuse being particular high points. Socialist feminism has forced Marxism to recognize that it is often in the most personal or apparently non-political settings that ideology gets most purchase.[59] Nevertheless, the hallmark of a materialist approach is that ideas do not float free of a social and historical context; they are produced by human animals in society, intimately tied up with the social practice of language and, in the final analysis, are constrained in their influence and application by the economic base of society.

The criticism of idealism has a contemporary feel. Since at least the global financial crisis of 2007–8, and especially since the 2016 Brexit Referendum and the election of Donald Trump in the same year, it has been a liberal commonplace that electorates are stupid or have shot themselves in the foot by poor electoral choices. It is particularly important, on this view, to defer to "experts" (if ever there were an ideologically loaded category, especially around economic issues, this is it). If only we (well, not "we", never *we*: they) had listened to the experts, Britain would not have voted to leave the EU. The key enemy for this form of contemporary liberalism is *populism*: the loose category captures any politics which mobilizes large numbers of people and appeals to such non-cerebral phenomena as emotions or senses of identity. It also blithely elides left-wing anti-capitalism with the kind of hard-right politics which is always capitalism's last defence against crisis, leaving only the sensible, rational, centre occupied by the likes of Emmanuel Macron, Hillary Clinton and Tony Blair. *Geist*, for this contemporary reworking of Hegel, comes to perfect self-realization in the *Guardian* weekend supplement. History, it seems, ends not with a bang, but with a whimper.

This is pure idealism in Marx's sense. From the perspective of his politics of working-class self-emancipation, moreover, we can see just why it is so damaging. Quite apart from the manner in which anti-populism represents the working class—a mass in danger of bringing disaster upon us all, in need of education and careful monitoring—it writes class itself out of the script of history. Instead of seeing the present politics of Western democracy in terms of struggles framed by the 2008 crisis, and the subsequent attempts to restore capitalist profitability through austerity, we are served ideal alternatives: there is a failure of trust in institutions, the electorate are unequipped for complex decision-making. The real, material forces at work in history get overlooked in favour of observations which could almost be made at any time, in any place. Similarly, the crucial differences between the class alignments and compositions of, say, Jeremy Corbyn's 2015 Labour leadership bid in the UK and Donald Trump's 2016 presidential campaign in the US get dismissed in favour of a uniform diagnosis of populism. Politics itself is depoliticized.[60]

Now, there is no reason why Christians need to sign up to idealism. To that extent Marxist materialism presents no problems for Christianity. However, the kind of idolatrous views of God we encountered in the discussion of atheism have a habit of coming back and making trouble. "History is in God's hands"; "God acts in history"—all of these and similar assertions are perfectly ordinary things for a Christian to say, and they express an orthodox trust in divine providence. The problem comes when we read them as statements about a super-being who causes things to happen instead of them being caused by material human beings. As we saw earlier, there is a pull towards idolatry in our thinking about God. Similarly, we find ourselves dragged towards hearing "History is in God's hands" as, for example, "History is in God's hands, and so is not determined by economic factors". At this point we are left with a theological version of idealism—what lies behind history is fundamentally mental, albeit that it is a *divine* mind. There are ample reasons, both political and theological, to resist this.[61]

Materialism and religious life

According to historical materialism the whole panoply of human institutions and systems of thought are conditioned and constrained by the economic base. In particular then, churches and their theology are conditioned by the economic base. Oughtn't this to cause problems for would-be Christian Marxists? Those conservative church authorities who took a dislike to Latin American liberation theology, especially the work of Brazilian theologian Leonardo Boff, during the 1980s certainly thought so.[62] It was one thing for liberation theologians to use Marxist tools to study society in general. It was quite another thing for those theologians to apply those methods to the Church itself, and it earned them a rebuke.[63]

Christian life and proclamation has, of necessity, something of a high self-opinion. Depending on where one falls within the confessional spectrum, and within the range of theologies in one's own church, the Church might be understood as an authoritative sign of God's coming kingdom, or as a community subject to the divine command to proclaim the gospel, or as a uniquely divinely authorized servant of humankind.[64] Then again, Christian talk about God is somehow understood as concerning, interpreting, and passing on God's saving self-communication to humankind. It cannot seem anything other than deflating to hear it for the first time suggested that the Church is shot through with the class divisions (and divisions of sex, race and sexuality) which characterize the societies in which it exists, that its proclamation is subject to the same economic conditioning as any other human cultural activity.

Yet how could it be otherwise? If the Church is to be a human institution, and the words spoken in its name, human words, then the usual conditions applying to human institutions and language (which is, of course, itself a particular kind of, and especially important, human institution)[65] will apply in these cases. From a Marxist perspective, therefore, Christian life and thought is susceptible to a materialist understanding, which aims to show, amongst other things, how economic factors constrain and direct its shape and content.

Is this a problem? It needn't be, in spite of the bluster directed at those liberation theologians who were indecent enough to raise the issue. The reason there might be thought to be a problem is that scripture is claimed as the word of God, church tradition as guided by God, the life of the Church as coming from God. Yet to the extent that these things are subject to causal influence from the material world (in the form of the economic base), it might be thought, they cannot be brought about by God. As soon as the view has been articulated, we can see that it is just a version of the Feuerbachian trade-off we encountered in the previous chapter: effects can only be attributed to divine agency to the extent that they are not attributed to a non-divine agency. We have seen that Marx rejects this trade-off (in his case, in the name of a socialist future) and that Christians ought to reject it. So the availability of materialist explanations of features of the Church and its life ought not to worry Christians.

A parallel might help get things clear: mainstream Christianity, following the Council of Chalcedon (451 CE), holds that the one person Jesus Christ is both truly human and truly divine. The temptation to understand Christ's divinity as being at the expense of his humanity, that he was somehow less than human, say, or merely God disguised as a human being, or that he lacked a properly human psychology, is ruled out by this mainstream. Chalcedon insists that the union of divine and human natures in Christ in no way takes away the "distinction of the natures" and, in particular, therefore, that he is "like us in all things except sin".[66]

Christ is human in exactly the same way that we are; yet his humanity is not an obstacle to his divinity, something which needs to be held in tension with it, or an unfortunate imposition in spite of which something of his divinity manages to shine through. It is rather precisely *through* Christ's humanity that the word of God is communicated to human beings. Against this mainstream view stands opposed *docetism*, the view, condemned as heretical, that Christ only appears to be fully human, but is in fact less than that. Now, undoubtedly much living Christianity is docetist in practice (just observe the shudders when it is suggested that Jesus, like every human being, had a sexual nature), but to that extent it dissents from the creeds and councils most Christians claim as authoritative. Jesus' humanity is just like ours. And that of course means that it was the object of social conditioning. Jesus, as a human being, could not have had views about second-wave feminism or quad core processing, simply because the material conditions in which he lived meant that questions about these things could not so much as arise. Moreover, Jesus belonged to a definite social class, had definite economic interests, and had a potential for acting in the world that was constrained and empowered by economic factors. All of this follows simply from his being human; Marxist materialism serves to bring this to our attention. The Christian position is not to deny any of this, but rather to insist that in and through this limited, conditioned, human being, God's word is spoken.

If Christians at least try to avoid being docetist with respect to Christ, docetism with respect to the *Church* is alive and well. The Church is, on the face of it, very obviously a human institution, a collection of human beings, with structures and a shared life. However, exalted claims are made for it: it is "the People of God" and "the Mystical Body of Christ", for instance.[67] Those conservative churchmen (and they *were* men) who opposed the liberation theologians turning critical attention to the Church feared that they were playing down this divinely given aspect of the Church by treating it as just another human organization. If the only way to ensure the status of the Church is to exempt it from the usual norms governing human societies, goes the implicit reasoning of this line of thought, so be it. Yet this conclusion is no more compulsory here than it was in the case of Christology (the theological understanding of the person of Jesus): the Church can be understood as both divine in origin and purpose, and yet a fully human organization, and the former because the latter. It is only if we start from a position where God and humanity compete for agency that this understanding is ruled out. And it is a recurring theme in this book that we shouldn't start from this position.

What does the thoroughly human and historical nature of the Church and Christian doctrine mean for the politically engaged Christian? First and foremost, it means that the *criticism of theology* and the *criticism of church life* are part and parcel of what it is to be a left-wing Christian. Theology, by which I mean not simply academic theology, but day-by-day Christian talk about God, whether from the pulpit or in the living room, is not magically exempt from Marx's insistence that the dominant ideas in any society are the ideas of the ruling class. There is a valuable job to be done in identifying the ways in which theologies serve the cause of capitalist exploitation and challenging them accordingly. Unfortunately for the would-be critic ideological complicity is not always as obvious as in the notorious verse from the hymn *All Things Bright and Beautiful*:

> The rich man in his castle,
> the poor man at his gate.
> God made them high and lowly,
> and ordered their estate.

Church life, the day-to-day practice of Christian communities, is also vulnerable to criticism along similar lines. This might be less obvious. But think: how does immersion in any given church community constrain the experience or direct the political ideas of a member? How does it play into nostalgic ideas of community, or ideas of the nation (think, for instance, about the observation of Remembrance Sunday)? At a larger scale, how might the relationship of the Church of England to the British State, or concordats between the Catholic Church and other nation states, limit the political horizons available within it, and so serve to bolster the *status quo*? There is much here to which criticism should be applied.

Materialism and Christian doctrine[68]

So far I've argued that Marxist materialism is compatible with Christian faith. As we come to the end of this chapter, however, I want to suggest more. There are good reasons from within Christian doctrine itself to embrace the characteristic materialist emphasis on human beings as material, social, animals. For Marx, we are not, at root, isolated individual animals, but social through and through; indeed our very individuality, our capacity to believe and desire, to form significant plans and understand ourselves as part of a narrative, depends on our possession of that most social of things, a language. Nor are we minds that happen to inhabit bodies; we are material beings. For all that there is a lot wrong with the desire to reduce every thought and experience down to neurons firing, as does a good deal of popular science writing today and as, in their own way, did those Marx criticized for being "vulgar materialists",[69] it does not follow that we ought to postulate some kind of mental or spiritual "inner self", isolated from the material world and perhaps immune from social conditioning. Instead we should insist that human beings are thinking animals, and that our animality provides us with the means by which we think (not least because our bodily nature is tied up with our capacity to use language).

The chief opponents of this kind of view are very often, these days at least, either reductively scientistic or else religious.[70] The latter group suppose that religious people ought to believe in something called the soul, which is part of the human person (not a material part, like my spleen, but a part nonetheless) and which is the conscious "bit" of me. Religion is concerned with "saving" this. Material things, including amongst other things our bodies, are less important.

The kind of soul-saving religion which results from this picture of the human being is ideological through and through. Those Christians who buy into it will focus on getting their soul to heaven (a process which is very often understood in a thoroughly individualistic fashion, as to do with "my personal relationship with Jesus", and not with the kind of agenda suggested in the first chapter of Luke's Gospel: "he has filled the hungry with good things, and the rich he has sent away empty").[71]

None of this sits well with Christian orthodoxy, and it is testimony to the ideological entrapment of a lot of popular theology, that the idea that Christian attention ought to focus on the spiritual (where this is a distinct region of reality)[72] has such currency. Credal Christianity affirms the createdness of the material order (which, according to one of the creation myths Christianity shares with Judaism, God sees as good),[73] it holds that God has become incarnate in that material order—eating, drinking, sharing life with others—that he was raised bodily and that the final destination of humankind is both bodily and social. It has, historically, talked of the soul, but there are ways of understanding this talk that are solidly anti-dualistic. Following Aristotle, Aquinas thought of the human soul as the form of a rational animal, that which structures matter as a particular kind of organism, capable of meaning. To say of someone that they have a soul, in this sense, is just to say that they are a living animal of a particular kind, and so amongst other things bodily. For Aquinas "my soul is not me", and if I am to be redeemed that redemption must be bodily.[74] All in all this sits considerably better with Marxist materialism than it does with the output of most televangelists.

CHAPTER 3

The Church and Revolution

Many Christians can come to agree with Marx in broad outline on a range of issues. There is a lot wrong with capitalism, these people will concur; society ought not to be run for private profit. No doubt, they will further admit, there are resources in Marx that can help us understand the world in order to change it: his class analysis of society, his pioneering work on the criticism of ideology, and the economics of *Capital* being cases in point. Where, ironically, a lot of people will refuse to follow Marx is in the area to which he dedicated his life and which his writings were intended to support: his politics.

Marx was a revolutionary. His political activity was focused on organizing the agency he believed to be capable of the revolutionary transformation of capitalist society, the working class. For the majority of even left-wing Christians, following Marx in this is a step too far. Revolution is violent, it involves division and hatred. It is the very opposite of the attitude towards life and the world presented in the Gospels.

In this chapter I want to cause problems for complacent dismissals of revolutionary politics. That doesn't mean that I don't think that there is a tension between the Christian vision of the kingdom of God and revolutionary politics. I think there is a tension; but it is just the tension that comes from living in a world awash with exploitation and oppression, and that we have to live with it, whilst also working to change the world.

Marx and Marxists on revolution

Before thinking about whether Marxist revolutionary politics can be reconciled with Christian faith, we would do well to get some clarity about how Marx and subsequent Marxist tradition understand revolution. In the first place, it ought to be acknowledged that whilst for contemporary readers the word "revolution" conjures up images of violent confrontation, of *Les Misérables*-style barricades or heroic guerrilla fighters, for Marx revolution is in the first place a matter of the depth of a social transformation rather than the means by which it is brought about. Revolution changes the relations of production, and in so doing transforms society. In the circumstances of capitalism, revolution would involve the end of the ownership of the means of production by the bourgeoisie. Marx writes relatively little about this process. He is clear that it is the working class that must bring about revolution; he writes of the "self-conscious, independent movement of the immense majority in the interests of the immense majority".[75] The tragic history of Stalinism, of bureaucracies and generals claiming to take power *on behalf of* the working class throughout Eastern Europe, bears witness to the wisdom of Marx's majoritarian focus. (It also deserves recognition at a time when it is fashionable in left-wing circles to celebrate marginal or minority status, that Marx invests his hope in the mass of ordinary people.) The lines with which the *Communist Manifesto* pits the working class against capital are amongst Marx's best known:

> The Communists disdain to conceal their views and aims. They openly declare that their ends can be attained only by the forcible overthrow of all existing social conditions. Let the ruling classes tremble at a Communistic revolution. The proletarians have nothing to lose but their chains. They have a world to win.
>
> Workers of All Countries, Unite![76]

Much revolutionary activity, that is activity aimed at preparing the working class to challenge bourgeois ownership of the means of production, is a million miles from the stuff of barricades and rifles. Socialists in the Marxist tradition have, in the usual course of things, viewed their task as being to further working-class consciousness—to help people develop a sense of themselves as a class with interests opposed to those of capital—and to bolster that class's self-confidence. This has largely been a matter of work within trade unions, political parties, and community campaigns and, whatever heroic imagery might attach to revolutionary politics, is not infrequently dull. These days if you sign up to a Marxist group in the industrialized West, you are far more likely to end up editing newsletters in Word than fleeing to the hills under cover of darkness. In particular, the mainstream of Marxist tradition from Marx and Engels onwards, and including authors as otherwise diverse as Luxemburg and Trotsky, has not shied away from involvement in electoral politics. Of course, it doesn't think that capitalism can be done away with by electoral means alone. The nature of the change required is too deep and the grip of the bourgeoisie too tight for that. Since, however, any movement towards the revolutionary transformation of society must start from society as it is now, the revolutionary will look for the points of potential intervention, the flashes of militancy, and the places where political ideas are being discussed. In the usual course of things, she will be doing the same kinds of things as her non-revolutionary leftist counterparts, and it might appear that the Christian has no better reason to criticize one than the other.

The crucial difference is summed up in a phrase already quoted from the *Communist Manifesto*, "the forcible overthrow of all existing social conditions". That this overthrow must, in the end, be forcible, even if it begins with, say, the election of a socialist government is a conclusion which results from Marx's wider analysis of society. The vast superstructural weight of the state is not, on the kind of analysis we saw in *The German Ideology*, a neutral mechanism ready to be taken up by whoever happens to win an election for whatever end. It is a means by which the ruling class rule, an edifice which functions to enable capital to continue exploiting the working class. In the *Manifesto*, Marx and Engels say that the "executive of the modern state is nothing but a committee for managing the common affairs of the whole bourgeoisie".[77] If this expresses a Marxist understanding of the *function* of the state, Lenin's account of "special bodies of armed men" as central to the exercise of state power lays out how that function is exercised.[78]

A lot can be achieved short of the revolutionary transformation of society—in *Capital* Marx discusses the fight to shorten the working day approvingly. But, when pushed to the limits of its existence, the capitalist state will deploy those armed bodies in its defence (as well as the vast resources of the media, capitalist political parties and so on, being used in the war for public opinion). In the twenty-first-century industrial world, which at the moment seems a long way from socialist transformation being even the topic of a sensible question, all this talk of revolutionary and counter-revolutionary violence can sound frankly unhinged. Yet it is important to be clear both why Marxism thinks that the transition to socialism will be met with violence, and that any violence it countenances in that context is, in essence, defensive. On this James Connolly, arguing against the anti-socialist lectures of a Jesuit, Father Kane of Dublin, deserves quoting at length:

> [W]e are not so childish as to imagine that the capitalist class of the future will shrink from the shedding of the blood of the workers in order to retain their ill-gotten gains. They shed more blood, destroy more working class lives every year, by the criminal carelessness with which they conduct industry and drive us to nerve-racking speed, than is lost in the average international war. In the United States there are killed on the railroads in one year more men than died in the Boer War on both sides. When the capitalists kill us so rapidly for the sake of a few pence extra profit it would be suicidal to expect that they would hesitate to slaughter us wholesale when their very existence as parasites was at stake. Therefore, the Socialists anticipate violence only because they know the evil nature of the beast they contend with. But with a working class thoroughly organized and already as workers in possession of the railroads, shops, factories and ships, we do not need to fear their violence. The hired assassin armies of the capitalist class will be impotent for evil when the railroad men refuse to transport them,

the miners to furnish coal for their ships of war, the dock labourers to load or coal these ships, the clothing workers to make uniforms, the sailors to provision them, the telegraphists to serve them, or the farmers to feed them. In the vote, the strike, the boycott and the *lockout exercised against the master class*, the Socialists have weapons that will make this social revolution comparatively bloodless and peaceable, despite the tigerish instincts or desires of the capitalist enemy, and the doleful Cassandra-like prophecies of our critic.[79]

Connolly himself was shot at dawn by British soldiers in the aftermath of the 1916 Easter Rising.

McCabe—class struggle and Christian love

Herbert McCabe's classic essay "The Class Struggle and Christian Love" is an important contribution to thinking through how Christian engagement with revolutionary politics, of the sort described above, might be justified.[80] McCabe takes seriously the argument that Christians ought to be opposed to struggle and violence; these things do not belong to the fullness of God's kingdom. In response, he doesn't seek to talk his imagined critic out of a preference for non-violence. Rather, he draws our attention to the fact that capitalist society is already beset with tensions and oppositions. The most basic of these is laid out by McCabe in the standard Marxist fashion:

> On [the] fundamental difference between worker and employer the whole class system rests. The worker is whoever by productive work actually creates wealth. The employer is not simply anyone who makes overall decisions about what work shall be done and how; he is the one who takes the surplus wealth created by the worker and uses it (in his own interests of course) as capital. Capitalism is just the system in which capital is accumulated for investment, in their own interests, by a group of people who own the means of production and employ large numbers of other people who do not own the means of production but produce both the wealth they receive back in wages and the surplus wealth which is used for investment by the owners.[81]

It is not the case that capitalist societies are peaceable havens of human co-existence, troubled only by the possibility of revolutionary troublemaking. Rather, these societies are intrinsically antagonistic, since the interests of the vast majority of people are diametrically opposed to, and can only be satisfied at the expense of, the interests of those who own and control the means of production. So, says McCabe:

> [T]he class war is intrinsic to capitalism. It is part of the dynamic of the capitalist process itself. It's not as though somebody said: 'Let's have a class struggle, let's adjust the imbalance of wealth by organising the poor workers against the rich capitalists'. Nothing of the kind. The tension and struggle between worker and capitalist is an essential part of the process itself.[82]

This is indeed unsatisfactory from the perspective of Christian ethics, thinks McCabe. We do not flourish best if we are always in conflict with our fellow human beings. In particular, if we are in such a situation then we can at best imperfectly live out Christ's invitation to a life of love. Whatever invitations to social peace might be issued from pulpits and newspapers, we cannot simply opt out of the pervasive conflict by an act of willpower (to suppose otherwise, thinks McCabe, would be to make Christianity into an "ideal theory", failing to reflect human reality). In a society characterized by class conflict, as of necessity any capitalist society is, there is no neutral position available. If one fails to take sides explicitly, one sides with the *status quo*, and so with the ruling class.

Since participation in class struggle cannot be avoided, what should Christians do? According to McCabe they should side with that combatant whose victory in the class struggle would mean its cessation and with it the end of class society, the working class. Does this mean that Christianity fails to be relevant as a guide to action for the Christian who takes McCabe's advice and sides with the working-class movement? By no means. McCabe thinks that fidelity to the Christian gospel will be manifest in the *way* in which a Christian revolutionary lives out her commitment to the better world. Such a person's life will be informed by the teaching of Jesus, and especially by the Sermon on the Mount.

This does not mean, as we have already seen, that she will avoid conflict. This is simply impossible. Nor does it even mean, as many might be tempted to think, that she will be committed to non-violence. On this issue McCabe takes a thoroughly traditional just-war approach, extending it to the case of a just revolution, and wryly noting the dismay church people who are quite happy to house regimental memorials in their buildings and observe military commemorations show about "violence", but only when the violence is not done on behalf of the powerful and wealthy.

What McCabe means by the Christian revolutionary's living according to the teachings of Jesus is summed up nicely by his assertion that they will be "loving, gentle, unprovoked to anger". If the description is not one conventionally associated with a revolutionary activist, that is not because McCabe advocates a watered-down radicalism made safe for the Christian gospel. Instead, he takes the gospel to be the best guide to living through the tensions and frustrations which attach to political action in a world where the very structures and forces which render such action necessary make it difficult to engage in it with human integrity:

> Who, after all, wants a comrade in the struggle who is an arrogant, loudmouthed aggressive bully? The kind of person who jumps on the revolutionary bandwagon in order to work off his or her bad temper or envy or unresolved conflict with parents does not make a good and reliable comrade. Whatever happened to all those 'revolutionary' students of 1968? What the revolution needs is grown-up people who have caught on to themselves, who have recognized their own infantilisms and to some extent dealt with them—people in fact who have listened to the Sermon on the Mount.[83]

McCabe further thinks that the revolutionary who is a Christian ought to be committed to forgiving her enemies. This will, not unreasonably, be met with concern by many Marxists, fearful of premature reconciliation serving to defuse necessary conflict. Surely a worker who forgives her boss for years of real-terms pay cuts is not going to then join in strike action against that boss. Eminently insightful in the light of currently dominant understandings of forgiveness, which have been criticized by feminists amongst others, this misses how McCabe (and arguably the mainstream of Christian tradition) thinks about the matter. For him, to forgive one's enemy is to refuse to be bitter or vindictive against them, it is to wager on a future in which I might live alongside my enemy peaceably (thought about in Christian terms as the kingdom of God). It is emphatically not to abandon the struggle for a just and loving society, which will continue to pit me in antagonism against those capitalism makes into my enemies. This is of relevance to the next item on our agenda, how Marxist politics can be reconciled with life in the Church.

The unity of the Church

Social struggle might very well be unavoidable, but there is a particular implication of a Marxist approach to politics which both deserves special attention, and which finds echoes in conservative criticisms of liberation theology. Suppose (as well you might) that I am a Marxist Christian. Then week by week, day by day perhaps, I stand in church alongside people who might be my political enemies. I want these people, along with their plans and desires for our world, to be defeated. Yet by my actions during the liturgy I proclaim that they are my fellow citizens in the kingdom of God, people with whom I hope to spend an eternity of love. This is shown supremely by my receiving communion with my political enemies (it doesn't matter whether or not this is in the same church building or not, what matters is that we are all communicants)—the eucharist is regarded as a foretaste of the heavenly banquet, a "promise of future glory". This aspect of the reception of the eucharist is emphasized by the sharing of the sign of peace, a handshake (in England at least, a place not known for over-enthusiastic displays of warmth), prior to communion.[84] The unity of the Church is professed in the creed recited on Sundays and holy days, and reference is made to it in numerous prayers, liturgical and otherwise. How can someone committed to the political and social defeat of their fellow Christians go along with all of this?

The question is only deferred by pointing out, quite correctly, that there is no obvious agonizing about this matter on the part of right-wing Christians. There is no shortage of people who are prepared to vote for parties committed to enforcing immigration controls against those with whom they are in eucharistic communion, and it is a rare Christian CEO who worries that doing the best he can to curb wage growth sits ill with the fellowship he professes on Sundays. There is an apparent tension between the meaning of church life and the commitments of revolutionary politics, and the fact that reactionaries are subject to the same tension is no more comforting than the observation that one's enemy's lifeboat has a leak as well.

The tension is not merely apparent, in any case; it is real. My preferred way of thinking through it is in terms of the relationship between the Church and the kingdom of God. By the kingdom, or reign,[85] of God I do not mean simply some kind of after-death state for individual human beings (this is undoubtedly how the expression is used in many contemporary settings). Rather I have in mind the biblical sense of the expression: the complete restoration of the created world in accordance with the loving will of God. In this sense, the kingdom of God includes the redemption of the created world in its material and social aspects, the "new heaven and new earth" pictured in the book of Revelation, and the fulfilment of the creation's labour pangs described by Paul writing to the Roman Christians.[86]

The kingdom was, according to the synoptic Gospels at least,[87] the focus of Jesus' preaching and works—he announced the coming of the kingdom of God and showed by his works that the kingdom was present, healing the sick and breaking down the barriers that divide human beings. But now contemporary Christians might seem to have a problem: we hold that the kingdom of God has arrived with Jesus, but the slightest glance at a news website ought to convince us that we are a very long way from that kingdom indeed. Exploitation, war, racism and sexism are rife; at the personal level we suffer loss, sickness, and death. The birth-pangs of which Paul wrote are all too evident.

The usual, and in my view correct, response to this tension is to insist on the provisional nature of the kingdom. It has been inaugurated through the life, death and resurrection of Jesus, but does not exist in its fullness until what the New Testament writers call the *eschaton*, the end. Until then, we have to work for its coming and look for the signs of its presence. What is the role of the Church in all of this? Here an idea revived within Catholic theology in the run-up to the Second Vatican Council can help us: the Church is a sacrament of the kingdom of God. A *sacrament*, for these purposes, is a sign which makes present the thing signified. The life of the Church, of God's baptized people, together in faith, hope and charity,[88] is a sign of the coming kingdom in which all will be at peace and all oppression and suffering done away with. But our life is not simply a sign, in the way that my writing down "God's kingdom will come, and all will be well" might be simply a sign.[89] On the contrary, in the life of the Church, the kingdom of God is really present. This is most obviously the case when the Church celebrates the sacraments, the individual signs of the coming kingdom (in particular the eucharist, which anticipates that supper where all will be fed, to which people are gathered "out of every nation"),[90] when its members live together in a way that speaks of solidarity and acceptance, and when they work (individually or collectively) for peace and justice.

But there's the rub. As we've seen, genuine work for peace and justice cannot, in a capitalist world, avoid conflict. So the Christian who celebrates the liturgy and shares parish life with others from different social and political positions, and does so effectively and whole-heartedly, will, if she is also committed to doing away with the alienation and exploitation of capitalist society, come into real social conflict with those same people. There is a tension here, but it is simply the tension of living in an imperfect world before the kingdom is fully realized. The fullness of the kingdom is, for Christians, seen at the present only in signs, the Church and its sacraments being important cases.

Now none of this means that the Christian revolutionary is permitted simply to shrug her shoulders and say "oh well, it's not a perfect world" as she unleashes fury upon her political enemies. As I've noted McCabe as saying, the spirit of the Sermon on the Mount should permeate a Christian's engagement in politics. Still, even if our Christian revolutionary doesn't spend every hour of the day seething in resentment at the person who narrowly defeated her in an election, she still wishes that she had beaten that person, and plans to do so next time, as she does with her opponents in industrial struggles and so on. Some of these people will be members of the Church. At the end of the day, all of this is simply a reminder that the Church is not the kingdom. When the kingdom comes there will be no Church, and no need for political struggle.

The reactionary role of churches

Perhaps the most obvious problem with a Christian adopting Marxist politics is that churches and prominent Christians have been resolutely opposed to those politics for the entire period of Marxism's existence. With good reason the list at the beginning of the *Communist Manifesto* of those opposed to the communist movement in Europe includes the pope and describes the assorted anti-communists as a "holy alliance".[91] At crucial points in subsequent years the appeal to the Christian faithful to oppose "godless communism" has been an important weapon in the hands of the political right. The worry arises: aren't churches intrinsically reactionary institutions, whose role has always been—with honourable exceptions[92]—to side with the rich against popular movements?

McCabe once got into trouble for saying that the Church was obviously corrupt, but that this was no reason to leave it. This is basically my position on the present topic, with the word "corrupt" replaced by "reactionary". Organized Christianity has, for the greater part of its two millennia of existence, been lined up with the dominating classes. A particularly fateful moment was Christianity's shift in status under the Emperor Constantine the Great from a persecuted religion to one favoured by the Emperor himself. Since then, at least until relatively recently, the rulers of the Western world looked to Christianity for support and justified their own power in terms of it. Wars were fought, and the war dead memorialized, under the standard of the cross. Clergy could most often be relied upon to warn of the dangers of rebellion. Where there have been important exceptions, as there were in Latin America under the influence of liberation theology, a central component in the ensuing outrage has been precisely that the clergy in question were refusing to play their proper role in a respectable, "Christian" society.

How does a Christian favourable to my outlook deal with this fact of the reactionary allegiance of the churches? One answer can be found in the work of Rosa Luxemburg:

> And here is the answer to all the attacks of the clergy: the Social-Democracy in no way fights against religious beliefs. On the contrary, it demands complete freedom of conscience for every individual and the widest possible toleration for every faith and every opinion. But, from the moment when the priests use the pulpit as a means of political struggle against the working classes, the workers must fight against the enemies of their rights and their liberation. For he who defends the exploiters and who helps to prolong this present regime of misery, he is the mortal enemy of the proletariat, whether he be in a cassock or in the uniform of the police.[93]

In other words, socialism's issue is not with religious belief as such, but with institutional reaction. And to the extent that people in churches make themselves enemies of socialism, socialists themselves have no option but to return the favour. This, of course, calls our attention back to the tension in church life we looked at earlier in this chapter: the revolutionary Christian exists alongside and in communion with people who, in Luxemburg's term, are enemies of the proletariat.

More can be said than this, though. In particular, it is not necessary for Christians within churches adopting reactionary political positions to take these lying down. We can, and should, object to them. There is a need for what we might call *critical theology*, which takes on statements or practices which function ideologically to preserve power (appeals to "social peace", or premature appeals to the "common good"; ideas about sex, gender, or nationality which bolster sexism and racism etc.) and shows that scripture and tradition needn't be read in ways which support these. This is valuable not only in itself, as a witness to truth against ideological distortion, but can also help to peel people away from reactionary church positions. Religious organizations are not monoliths; they are themselves sites of material struggle and battles of ideas. It would be odd if those with sympathy for Marx's ideas within churches weren't involved in these battles.

CHAPTER 4

Ethics

What you have written up until this point is all very well, I can imagine (perhaps optimistically) a reader saying, but you've missed a vital point about religion. It is a sad fact that religion, and Christianity in particular, preaches a constrictive morality which hinders people's capacity to live fulfilled lives and subjects them to damaging levels of guilt. No person concerned with human emancipation, and, in particular, no Marxist, can condone religion.

The association between Christianity and guilt is widespread, and not without cause—thumb through a few paperbacks on "Christian living" in your nearest religious bookshop and it won't be hard to empathize with the sentiment expressed in William Blake's *The Garden of Love*:

> I went to the Garden of Love,
> And saw what I never had seen:
> A Chapel was built in the midst,
> Where I used to play on the green.

And the gates of this Chapel were shut,
And *Thou shalt not* writ over the door;
So I turn'd to the Garden of Love,
That so many sweet flowers bore.

And I saw it was filled with graves,
And tomb-stones where flowers should be:
And Priests in black gowns, were walking their rounds,
And binding with briars, my joys & desires.[94]

For the line of criticism present here, religion (specifically Christianity here) is a matter of rules ("thou shalt not"), and these rules strangle the human capacity to live fully. For Blake, Jesus is a romantic much like himself. As he has the devil say in *The Marriage of Heaven and Hell*:

[I]f Jesus Christ is the greatest man, you ought to love him in the greatest degree; now hear how he has given his sanction to the law of ten commandments: did he not mock at the sabbath, and so mock the sabbath's God? murder those who were murder'd because of him? turn away the law from the woman taken in adultery? steal the labour of others to support him? bear false witness when he omitted making a defense before Pilate? covet when he pray'd for his disciples, and when he bid them shake off the dust of their feet against such as refused to lodge them? I tell you, no virtue can exist without breaking these ten

commandments; Jesus was all virtue, and acted from
impulse, not from rules.[95]

The only satisfactory response here is entire agreement
with Blake on two counts. First, that there are profoundly
damaging forms of morality which rob human beings
of agency and subject them to burdens which are
encountered as alien and external to them. Second,
that it is far better to do the right thing freely because
it arises from one's character ("virtue" in Blake's sense)
than it is to act out of desire to follow the law, whatever
that law may be. Someone who was "all virtue" would
indeed not require rules. On this point the great ethical
tradition coming down from Aristotle's *Nicomachean
Ethics* agrees (although it is more pragmatic than Blake
in allowing that those of us who are as yet far from being
all virtue will need rules).[96] My aim in this chapter is
to suggest that this tradition, known as *virtue ethics*,[97]
coheres well with both Marxism and Christianity and
provides a credible alternative to a certain kind of life-
draining morality which is too often a feature of both.

According to what I will term *moralism*:

- Ethical life is a matter of following rules.
- We experience these rules as coming somehow
  from "outside" ourselves.
- These rules constrain us, taking the form mainly
  of prohibitions.

- Punishment is the appropriate response to someone's not following these rules.

It's easy to see that the fire-and-brimstone preacher is a moralist. So too, however, is a good proportion of the left, in turn reflecting a wider societal fixation with moralism: (Did *you* stay sober for all of October? Did you see what such-and-such a celebrity did on live TV? Sign this petition for them to be taken off air!).[98] Increasingly, and I think that the growth of social media at a time when genuine collective political action was at a low point was a key factor here, the "calling out" of individuals for their presumed political deviations, accompanied by exhortations to "self-criticism" on the part of those who remain, features heavily in left-wing culture. My own experience is that this trend has made parts of the left, particularly around university campuses, highly unpleasant places to be. The fact that elements of the far right have noticed this, using it as a stick with which to beat both the left and academia, is no good reason to deny the reality of left moralism, but all the more reason to undermine it in favour of structures conducive to solidarity and political community.[99]

Unpleasant though it may be, though, what is wrong with moralism? Might it not just be the case that doing what we ought to do is unappealing, but that we ought to do it anyway? The problem with the line lurking beneath this questioning is one about *motivation*. Unless it is good for *me* to do something, it is unclear that there is a good answer to the question why I ought to do it.[100] Of course, we should distinguish what is good for me from what immediately feels good, or seems easy—proper self-regard is different from selfishness—still, unless a morality can offer some genuine reason why a person ought to do the right thing it has not got as far as first base. "Because God has decreed it" or "OMG, you just don't do that—educate yourself" are neither of them adequate answers to the question why we should do the right thing. Neither of them offers reasons in terms which are capable of motivating us to follow a line of action, reasons having to do with ourselves rather than an external agency. They are, then, impressively dressed up ways of avoiding the question. Can we do better?

Virtue

There is an ancient ethical tradition for which, far from being constituted by following the rules, a good life just is a happy life. For sure the notion of happiness in play here is one for which being *really* happy is different from simply having pleasurable experiences, or having fun, but this distinction is part of how we ordinarily talk about one another and not simply the invention of some philosopher—"I worry about Paul, he's going out every night and travelling lots, but I don't think he's really happy" is a perfectly intelligible thing to say. The problem with Paul here is that his life lacks a certain kind of shape (people might talk of narrative structure or meaning) and that so much of his potential—to be creative, to form meaningful relationships, and so on—is unrealized. Perhaps a better word than "happiness" is "fulfilment"; the Greek word is *"eudaimonia"*, or "good living". For Aristotle *eudaimonia* is the characteristic of a good human life. Human living is done well when the human being in question is fulfilled. And, thinks Aristotle, there is no good answer to that question why fulfilment is the thing we seek. If you think that this is a good question, you simply don't understand what fulfilment is.[101] Virtues, then, are just the skills for living that make up such a good life. A fulfilled person just is just, kind, wise, and so on. And if it seems odd to talk about wisdom in terms of skill, that is because the terminology has been taken over by HR departments whose aim is profit rather than fulfilment.

The suggestion that fulfilment is the most desirable end of human life is far more attractive than moralism's dour insistence that we follow the rules, but does it provide enough material for anything like systematic thought about ethics? Elizabeth Anscombe, the philosopher whose essay *Modern Moral Philosophy* revived virtue ethics in the mid-twentieth century, was doubtful about the immediate prospects. In the paper she dispatches several versions of moralism. She prefaces it with the assertion that "it is not profitable for us at present to do moral philosophy". Why? According to Anscombe, because philosophy in 1950s Britain lacked an "adequate philosophy of psychology".[102] By this she meant what is more usually called a moral psychology, an account of human beings, our motivations and capacity for acting in the world. In Anscombe's later career she'd go some way towards filling this gap with her ground-breaking book *Intention*.[103]

To understand what a fulfilled life looks like we need to understand ourselves. I want to suggest that, each in its own way, both Marxism and Christianity can contribute to such understanding. Apart from anything else both stress an aspect of human existence shared with the classical virtue tradition but often downplayed by contemporary ethics: its fundamentally social nature. For Aristotle, it is inconceivable that we can think about ethics without thinking about politics, the life of society (for Aristotle, this meant the life of the city state, or *polis*). On the one hand, it is within society that my character is formed, that I will learn whichever virtues I possess (or for that matter vices: capitalist society, for example, teaches us to be competitive); on the other, many virtues consist in the capacity to contribute to our shared life together. The virtue of justice is an obvious case. So tightly bound does he take the social and the ethical to be that when, at the start of his *Nicomachean Ethics*, Aristotle talks of a field of study concerned with the human good, he calls it not *ethics* (as you might expect), but *politics*.[104]

According to virtue ethics, in vivid contrast to moralism:

- Ethical life is a matter of flourishing.
- The motivation to flourish is basic to us.
- Rules, and in particular prohibitions, have a secondary place to flourishing.
- In order to understand how we might flourish, we need to understand ourselves better as social, rational, animals.

Virtue and Marx

How do virtue ethics and Marxism relate to one another? The question of what Marx thought about morality is a vexed one.[105] At several points in his writing he is severely critical of morality. In texts like *The Critique of the Gotha Programme* he takes barbed aim at moral critics of capitalism. But it is difficult to imagine more vehement, apparently ethical, denunciations of capitalism than those found in Marx's own writings. At least part of the way out of this conundrum is to recognize that Marx's criticisms of morality were directed against versions of what I've called moralism. Removing consideration of the human good from any social or political context, these functioned ideologically. In particular, they made possible an abstract and moralizing "utopian" socialism which contrasted unfavourably with Marx's own "scientific" socialism.[106]

Progress can be made by bringing virtue ethics into the picture. If it is possible to have intellectual commitments concerning what is good for human beings without being a moralist, as the virtue ethicists claim, then Marx could have had this sort of commitment without being inconsistent. Arguing for the correctness of virtue ethics is ambitious beyond the length of this book, but there is a lot to be said for the view that Marx adhered to a form of Aristotelian ethics in his early years (and, so, for those of us who think that his early ideas directed his entire work, that Marx retained this adherence).[107]

In outline, an Aristotelian ethic holds that to be fulfilled as a human being is to realize one's nature. There just are certain ways of being which will give rise to human flourishing, and others which are antithetical to it. Ethics is, then, concerned with our nature, and so amongst other things with the facts that we are animal, embodied, and social. This way of looking at the ethical terrain is entirely compatible with the view—which Marx held—that human nature changes as human societies are transformed. The needs of a twenty-first-century person living under capitalism are manifestly not the same as those of a thirteenth-century peasant, who wouldn't be the least bit socially disadvantaged in lacking access to Wi-Fi; yet those needs are still in an important way *given*. I cannot change the fact that I need electricity to flourish simply by an act of will. The Aristotelian outlook is not compatible with those, sometimes found in universities with the dated label "postmodernist" attached to them, who deny that there is any such thing as human nature. Even if this were not a very short book, I do not consider this view credible enough to bother arguing against it.[108]

To be of any use or interest an Aristotelian ethics needs to tell us something about human nature; what is it, and how can it be fulfilled? In his early manuscript *On Alienated Labour*, Marx does exactly this.[109] Marx writes about the human species-being; he gets the expression from Feuerbach and uses it to refer to the nature we have as part of a biological species which understands itself as being part of a species.[110] Although the terminology is a world away, the Feuerbachian–Marxian understanding of human beings as species-being is in fact very close to Aristotle's use of "rational animal" to describe our species. And both Aristotle and Marx think that what a good human life looks like is conditioned by the fact that we are animals. If we do not take our finite, fragile, nature into account, for example, we will come unstuck, notwithstanding the insistence of management gurus that "the sky's the limit". Yet both Aristotle and Marx also insist that we are never simply animals. We are animals whose interaction with the world, with other human beings and with ourselves is always that of reasoning, language-using, creatures. Marx puts the point nicely in the first volume of *Capital*:

> A spider conducts operations that resemble those of a weaver, and a bee puts to shame many an architect in the construction of her cells. But what distinguishes the worst architect from the best of bees is this, that

the architect raises his structure in imagination
before he erects it in reality.[111]

The human species-being finds fulfilment in creatively
transforming the world around us, making things to
provide for our needs (whether those needs are "from
the stomach or the fancy", as Marx puts it: producing a
graphic novel might fulfil someone's species-being just
as might cooking a meal). If you want some sense of
what a flourishing human being looks like for Marx, a
craftsperson, musician, or novelist probably provides the
best approximation (the Stalinist dystopia of identikit
workers engaged in tractor production is far from
Marx's vision: for him it is capitalism, not communism,
which enforces uniformity and stems creativity). If the
word "creative" has been annexed under late capitalism
as a description of a certain personality type, that is an
indictment of late capitalism. In the Marxian view we are
all, by nature, creatives. The problem is that capitalism
separates us from the possibility of fulfilling that nature.
To re-use a term we have already encountered, it renders
us *alienated*. I could be interacting with nature and
fulfilling my potential by building an eco-friendly chalet
from raw materials, say; in fact, I'm filling in yet another
survey for the HR department.

According to Marx the alienation of workers under
capitalism is fourfold (Marx also thinks that the
bourgeoisie are alienated, but the nature of that alienation
is different). Workers are alienated from the *products*

of our labour, whether individual or collective—we do not produce items for our own use or delight, but for an employer, typically to be sold on. We are alienated from our own capacity to be productive (our *"labour-power"* for Marx), since this is directed by our employer rather than according to our own projects or needs. The wider implications of this for the possibility of human happiness are presented memorably by Marx:

> [The worker's] labour is therefore not voluntary, but coerced; it is *forced labour*. It is therefore not the satisfaction of a need; it is merely a *means* to satisfy needs external to it. Its alien character emerges clearly in the fact that as soon as no physical or other compulsion exists, labour is shunned like the plague. External labour, labour in which man alienates himself, is a labour of self-sacrifice, of mortification. Lastly, the external character of labour for the worker appears in the fact that it is not his own, but someone else's, that it does not belong to him, that in it he belongs, not to himself, but to another. Just as in religion the spontaneous activity of the human imagination, of the human brain and the human heart, operates on the individual independently of him—that is, operates as an alien, divine or diabolical activity—so is the worker's activity not his spontaneous activity. It belongs to another; it is the loss of his self.[112]

The idea of religious alienation, which we met in the first chapter, is applied to good effect as a point of comparison for the worker's loss of self in her work. The third form of alienation Marx describes is from our *species-being*, from what it is to be properly human. We are, finally, alienated from *one another*: rather than producing collectively as part of a shared project over which we have control, we live as fragmented, individual workers, whose relationship to one another is by default one of competition.

The picture Marx paints of alienated labour is a vivid one and is rooted in a fundamental optimism about human creative capacities (which, many Marxist writers have suggested, we catch a glimpse of in art).[113] How does it fit together with virtue ethics? Virtue ethics, remember, thinks about the human good in terms of flourishing. To lend substance to the position, some account is needed of what human flourishing looks like. Marx provides at least part of such an account, and one that has a good deal of plausibility: through the free, rational, and social use of our collective powers we find fulfilment (just think back across your own life, haven't there been moments where something approaching this has been present, and doesn't that stand in contrast with much of your experience?) However, the way society is organized inhibits systematically this sort of flourishing. Hence in order to allow us to flourish, society must be transformed: ethics leads into politics.

In order to head off a likely objection, this does not entail that all moral constraints are off until the revolution (although some Marxists seem to have thought this). Consistently with everything that has been said in this section, a Marxist can agree with ordinary everyday judgements about right and wrong, good and evil—indeed if she doesn't, we might imagine that she doesn't mean the same thing by the word "good" as other people, and so might think her ethical condemnation of capitalism is talking past them—and she ought to try to be a good person, to show pity, to be just and wise, a good friend, and so on. The Marxist, however, has the advantage in two respects. Firstly, she can draw attention to a vitally important part of human existence, our working lives, where the prerequisites for flourishing are systematically denied us. Moreover, she can counter, even regarding ordinary everyday goodness—the pitying, being a friend and so on—capitalism grinds away at our capacity to be good, making us competitive, suspicious, acquisitive, shutting us up in the private spaces behind our front doors, wary of the outside world. We needn't agree with Adorno's judgement that there can be no right living in a wrong world to insist that under capitalism many possible human goods are stillborn.[114] The situation of human beings under capitalism is tragic: history has brought us to a point where there are so many possibilities for flourishing, yet that same history stops us from realizing them. The solution, thinks Marx, is to move history onwards.

Virtue and Christianity

What about Christianity? Surely here the rejection of moralism is a tall order. After all, within Christianity (and other religions, for that matter) rules seem central to the understanding of ethics. You only need to think of the Ten Commandments to see the plausibility of this line of thought. Even when Jesus in the gospels wants to sum up the law, he does so in terms of two commands—to love God and one's neighbour.[115] And even when subsequent Christian tradition wanted to stress a role for human reasoning in the sphere of morality, it did so in terms of a natural law, which has often been understood (as the term itself suggests) as a system of moral rules somehow built into the nature of things and accessible to human reason. And when people transgress, hasn't there as often as not been the threat of divine punishment? In short, isn't Christian ethics pure moralism?

On the contrary, a virtue ethical approach is not only possible within Christianity but is present in the thought of key Christian theologians and philosophers, notably Aquinas. I'll set the issue of punishment aside, simply agreeing that there has been an unhealthy fixation on this in much Christianity, and that a reorientation of emphasis is needed. On the question of rules, it is important to make a distinction between an ethics which *includes* rules and an ethics which is *focused on* rules. For the latter, what it is to be a good human being is to live in obedience to certain rules. This is an unattractively legalistic vision of what it is to be human and is rightly rejected. It does not follow, however, that rules have no place in the ethical life. For one less exacting approach, where ethics includes (but is not limited to) rules, what it is to be a good human being is to flourish. It's just that we can be helped towards the goal of flourishing by rules (whether these are absolute, or guidelines, or a combination of both). For many virtue ethicists rules function rather like stabilizers on a child's bicycle, guiding us whilst we get the hang of living until acting rightly becomes second nature (in Blake's phraseology, until we are "all virtue"). Rules train us, our behaviour, our desires, so that we become good people. This means, amongst other things, that being good is a social (and so a political) matter, since to follow a rule is to engage in a communal practice.

Rules, then, matter, but they are not what matters most in ethics. What matters most is flourishing. Countering objections to the effect that there is no shared goal of all human lives, Aquinas replies by quoting Augustine: "all agree in desiring the last end: which is happiness".[116] This is a much more agreeable take on the purpose of life than that of the moralists, and for virtue ethics rules are simply a means towards this desirable end. On this basis a Christian can read the tradition and the commandments without succumbing to moralism, and—importantly— she can agree with what has been said above about the role of social structures and institutions in aiding, or

stunting, human flourishing. She can further accept
Marx's insights about the importance of creativity and
the fact that this is stifled under capitalism. There seems
to be a solid basis for bringing Marxist and Christian
ethics close together under the shared umbrella of virtue
ethics, and of uniting both in opposition to moralism.

Where Christianity goes beyond any purely secular
virtue ethics is in announcing that human beings are no
longer solely capable of merely human flourishing.[117]
By a divine gift, present to us through the life, death,
and resurrection of Jesus, human beings are invited
to share in the life of God itself; it is open to us now
to flourish as divinely human beings. As with natural
human flourishing, this new way of being human has
virtues associated with it: faith, hope, and charity.[118]
Unlike the natural virtues these theological virtues
cannot be acquired by hard work and patient practice,
they are simply to be received as an undeserved gift.
The most human beings can do, according to orthodox
Christianity, is make themselves open to it. Of
course, politics is operative even here: different social
circumstances make it more or less easy to be open to
the offer of grace. One excellent reason for Christians
to oppose capitalism, in my view, is that it is a social
system that makes the offer of unconditional divine love,
beyond any need to compete for favours or prove one's
worth, appear nigh-on incomprehensible. If God doesn't
even want to see my CV before giving me a share in the
divine life, can it really be worth having?

It would be a problem for the position that someone can be both a Christian and a Marxist if the way of flourishing characterized by faith, hope, and charity were incompatible with ordinary human flourishing. And there is a temptation to think that this is so: isn't that what all the talk in John's Gospel about rejecting "the world" is all about? Moreover, isn't the experience of Christian life that to the extent that you seriously live out the kind of life commended in the Gospels, you will not only fail to flourish (in quite concrete ways, monetarily, career-wise, and so on), but you are likely to be thought profoundly odd and best avoided? The fact that Herbert McCabe's line "if you don't love, you will die; if you do love, they will kill you" carries such resonance suggests that something is up here.

These kinds of consideration can quickly lead people from a radical counter-cultural Christianity to an inward-looking sectarianism, so it is crucial to get clear about some distinctions. It is, of course, the case that trying to live in a way which makes the greatest least and recognizes the peacemakers as blessed is unlikely to go down very well in a world in which arms manufacturers get, to put it mildly, a bigger reward than peacemakers. But that is not because characteristically Christian ways of living conflict with human flourishing. Rather it is because societies founded on competition and violence are not compatible with human flourishing, whether that be the flourishing of Christians or their neighbours of other religions or none. Far from the experience of being out of step with dominant mores causing Christians to retreat into an ecclesiastical ghetto, it ought to cause us to seek out allies, "people of good will" in the standard Catholic phrase, who can help us fight for a world fit for human beings.

Aquinas writes that "grace does not destroy nature, but perfects it".[119] Whatever it is that God does for human beings through Jesus, it is not something that erases our underlying human nature, our species-being. Rather it builds on it and brings out new possibilities. There can be no fear, then, that in joining the socialist struggle against a world whose sole deity is profit, in the cause of human flourishing, the Christian is turning away from the kind of flourishing which ought to concern her. On the contrary, she is fighting for a world in which human co-existence in both nature and grace is more apparent and can be our focus without the economic competition, racism, and sexism which fracture our common life.

Human flourishing is a social endeavour. According to Christians, it will only be perfectly realized in the future reality known as the kingdom of God, in which we, in solidarity and fellowship with one another, enjoy the vision of God's glory. Regardless of one's religious beliefs, flourishing ought to be seen as a political matter, since the society we inhabit either facilitates or impedes our flourishing. Marx claims that capitalism is an impediment to flourishing because of alienation. Christians can agree with this and see moving beyond capitalism as related to (although not identical with) the coming of God's reign. In either case, we look forward to a future in which human flourishing is more abundant.

Conclusion

Graham Greene's comedic novella *Monsignor Quixote* describes the travels of the eponymous priest with the former communist mayor of his Spanish town, soon after the end of the Franco era. Their friendly, joking yet serious, discussion of the causes to which they have each committed their life runs through the novel, the lightness of touch with which it is presented somehow rendering approachable the enormity of the subject matter of their often-drunken debates. Quixote attempts to demonstrate the doctrine of the Trinity using three wine bottles, two of which are empty because of the evening's drinking: the explanation turns out to be heretical since the bottle representing the Holy Spirit is only half empty. Sancho, the mayor, succeeds in getting Quixote to read the *Communist Manifesto* (he is impressed with it, although not for the reasons Sancho might like). Each of them taunts the other with the failures of the tradition he inhabits, the Inquisition for one, Stalin for the other. These exchanges take place on a piecemeal basis, as the fancy takes the participants, against the backdrop of a deepening friendship and of shared adventure.

This serves well as an image of how I understand conversations between Christianity and Marxism. They are likely to be unsystematic, arising out of the need for clarity in particular situations or out of the questioner's fancy. They will most fruitfully surface within a framework of shared practical commitment: understanding where you are coming from is, if you and I are both intensely involved in some industrial struggle or political campaign, not an idle luxury, or mere intellectual goal; rather it is an imperative arising out of our common political life.

This is the approach I have found most useful in my own life. Here the conversations between Christianity and Marxism have been internal to my own commitments as well as with friends and comrades. It is present in the foregoing chapters to this extent: these are the topics which have come up when questions about Christianity and Marxism have been raised around me. My conviction that conversations about Marxism and Christianity ought to open the way for shared practice will have been apparent in my prioritizing clearing away barriers to such practice.

Not everyone sees matters this way. During the second half of the twentieth century, with governments claiming an allegiance to Marx ruling a fair amount of the world, and reform movements of various kinds sweeping through the Christian churches, there was much talk of a Christian–Marxist dialogue, seemingly modelled on the ecumenical dialogues then taking place between the churches. This dialogue was on a grand scale, aiming to bring two accounts of reality together with the purpose of resolution.[120] Speaking some years after the high-point of Christian–Marxist dialogue, Tony Benn made the religious parallel explicit:

> [A]s the ecumenical movement gathers momentum—and if it remains a mosaic and does not become a monolith—it should extend the range of its dialogue to embrace socialists and Marxists as well as Catholics, Protestants, Jews, Buddhists, and Muslims. And there is one compelling reason why it must.
>
> The technology of destruction at the disposal of mankind in modern weapons and the rocketry to deliver them must now require us all to open our hearts and minds to the inescapable need for neighbourly love on a global scale and then build the social, political, and economic institutions that can express it, bringing together those who now marshal themselves under different banners of religious and political faith.
>
> A holy war with atom bombs could end the human family for ever.[121]

That last chilling sentence is certainly true, and Benn was a great man. But the idea that Marxism is the same sort of thing as a religion, such that it could intelligibly be part of an ecumenism with religions, is a disastrous confusion which will not only stand in the way of the hoped-for dialogue but will bolster the kind of unattractive view of Marxism as a kind of scientific religion, a theory of everything, which got a hold in the Stalinist states. Marxism is not a religion, nor does its language or practice look in obvious danger of trespassing on religious turf. From a certain angle Marxism is a modest affair, severely limited in its remit: it is a highly specific practice, one of social criticism along with and as part of working-class struggle against capitalism. Christianity meanwhile is more obviously universal in its scope. It has something to say about everything, namely that each thing is created by God and that the world is redeemed in Christ; but as we saw when discussing atheism, to say that things stand somehow in respect of God is to run up against the failure of our language to say anything adequate of God. Compared to the specific, often vociferous, nature of Marxism, Christianity aspires to speak universally but hesitantly. The two are clearly not the same sort of thing. The temptation to suppose otherwise goes hand in hand with the temptation to set up the party, the leader, or dialectical materialism as gods.

This does not mean that serious points of disagreement and tension, as well as moments of shared insight and recognition of common ground, don't appear between Christians and Marxists. It is just that they are not of the predictable sort that occur between people disputing on the same territory: "you think that the labour theory of value is consistent, whereas I don't" or "you think that Christ has two distinct natures, human and divine, whilst I think that he was just a man." For as long as there are Christianity and Marxism, fruitful exchanges between the two will mirror Monsignor Quixote and his mayor.

I use the words "for *as long as* there are Christianity and Marxism" advisedly. Both Marxism and Christianity look towards their own abolition. Unlike the Starbucks corporation, say, which presumably aspires to be selling lattes even as the melting ice-caps cascade through the doors of its London branches, Christians and Marxists alike long for the conditions which necessitate the end of their existences. Both therefore require a genuine historical consciousness, open to the possibility of radical change and transformation, unthinkable for those who are confident that anything important that happens in the future will be describable on a bar chart. Marxists look forward to a working-class revolution, necessarily international, which will end capitalism, and with capitalism class society, and with class society Marxism as the movement which aims at its abolition. Christianity meanwhile looks forward to the fullness of the Reign of God, in which the human body itself will be transformed, death conquered finally, and all will live peaceably in the loving presence of God. In this state there will be no more need for religion, which anticipates the kingdom of God, and in its sacraments makes it present before its full manifestation. When Christianity's hope is fulfilled, Christianity will be no more. "I saw no temple in the city."[122]

Looking forward to the future is an art we cannot afford to lose. Whilst there is a good deal of discontent—with stagnant wages and austerity regimes, hawkish international policy, the mounting precarity of life, work and housing—this can so easily find an outlet in cynical resignation, or worse in the politics of the far-right. Fascism wants to make the future literally unthinkable, to transform the present into the battlegrounds and conquests of an imagined national past.[123] The kind of technocratic politics which is the expression of cynicism at the executive level, precisely because it can see no way beyond the present, clears the ground for far more sinister forces. Stand Hillary Clinton as a candidate; get Donald Trump as president.

The most immediate task, it seems to me, for Marxists and Christians alike is to *keep history open*. Perhaps the best thing Marxists can take from Christianity at this present time is simply a fragment of a Bible verse:

> Always be ready to make your defense to anyone who demands from you an accounting for the hope that is in you.[124]

Christians are bound to believe that the future is open, and that it is open in a way which demands hope as its response; their reason for hope is God's promise. Yet if a distinctive role for Christians is that of custodians of hope, it falls to Marxists to deliver the kind of corrective which prevents this hope degenerating into a too-easy optimism, or into a future-orientation so abstract that it has nothing to say to present struggles.[125] It is in the concrete, lived reality of industrial and political struggle that the seeds of a future free from exploitation and oppression are to be found. The Marxist tradition provides a way of looking at the world, in solidarity with and from the perspective of working-class self-organization, which enables sense to be made of the complexities of contemporary politics and society. We are given a way of reading the "signs of the times"; and these times certainly need that.

Marxism and Christianity, then, each have something to offer each other, just as—so I believe, or else I would not be writing this—each has something to offer the human race. I would be guilty of either deceit or naivety if I didn't follow this affirmation by acknowledging that the human race, particularly in the industrialized[126] West, doesn't seem particularly keen on taking on board the insights of either Christianity or Marxism. Yet it is at this point that another selling point of Marxism comes to the fore. One excellent reason to be a Marxist is that Marxism is able to account for its own failure.

Let me explain. The Marxist can look at the accelerating capitalism of recent years, under the management of political regimes generally termed *neo-liberal*, at the class struggles fought and won by the ruling class (in Britain the defeat of the 1984–5 Miners' Strike is of decisive importance), at the fragmentation of communities, the growth of individualism and the ideology of the entrepreneurial self (wanting to get ahead at every point, always on the look out to improve one's CV, one's "personal brand"); she can look at all these things and say that *of course* in these material and ideological circumstances Marxism will not flourish. This does not mean that Marxism's claims are false. Rather, to apply a biblical metaphor, the soil is not rich enough at the moment for the seed of Marxism to take. Human beings are not creatures of pure reason, and the circumstances in which an idea is encountered, and the practical consequences of its adoption, can play at least as much a part in determining whether it is adopted as factors on which its truth or falsity has a bearing.

The same considerations, of course, apply to Christianity. It is not difficult to see that the fragmentation of life under neo-liberalism is hardly conducive to Christian belonging and practice. Indeed, many of our contemporaries do not so much as inhabit a way of life in which the claims made by Christianity could make sense. Christian belief arises out of reflection on Christian practice, and Christian practice is communal. Make the life of the Church difficult, as does a society which disciplines us as workers with long hours and low security yet tempts us as consumers with a seemingly endless variety of routes to our own individual pleasure, and it will be entirely unsurprising that Christianity declines. It does not follow that people have found a new good reason to reject Christianity, as though the bones of Jesus had been found somewhere in Palestine.

One of the worst features of the present political moment is the rise of the smug liberal rationalist. According to this character whatever the problem— Trump, say, or Brexit—the root is human stupidity. The smug liberal rationalist, in his own estimation (he really is a *he*), sees his way clearly beyond the stupidity of the masses, and if only a sufficient number of people would listen to him, our salvation would be assured. All we need to do is what the smug liberal rationalist has done before us: *think*. It hardly needs to be said that, insofar as Marxism or Christianity enter the consciousness of our rationalist (the latter, at least, does for incarnations of the rationalist ranging from Richard Dawkins to a good number of comedians) they are taken to be prime examples of bad ideas, dogmas which could be expelled by the perfunctory remedy of thinking a little harder.

The Marxist and the Christian, sat to one side of the mainstage of contemporary political life, perhaps sharing a drink like Quixote and Sancho, may yet have the last laugh. The smug liberal rationalist is not, it turns out, a creature of sheer unsituated rationality; his ideas are themselves the perfectly explicable product of a particular age, serving identifiable interests, and appealing to definite, ideologically formed, self-understandings. If he seems ascendant at the moment, or at least the only realistic alternative to qualitatively worse reaction—nationalism and bigotry—then that is not because he has somehow triumphed in the arena of argument. It is rather that this is what you get if you concede to neo-liberalism the task of setting the boundaries for acceptable political dissent: a form of politics whose cerebral individualism appeals to the self-image of the informed consumer, the ideal subject of post-Thatcher society, and whose thoroughgoing machismo, albeit tempered these days by a professed sensitivity, witnesses to the ongoing complicity of patriarchy and capitalism. But neo-liberal capitalism has not always existed and will not always exist. And that means that the basis for contemporary rejection of Marxism and Christianity alike is historically transient.

The Marxist and the Christian look across at the smug rationalist liberal. He has only been on stage a few minutes, yet the beads of sweat are already appearing on his brow. He will not last forever. They clink their glasses, "our time will come". They might be right, but there are altogether more ugly characters waiting in the wings, eager to turn the ending of neo-liberalism to nationalist or other chauvinist ends.[127] The future depends on human action and human organization. Not even the most convinced Christian should deny that.

Notes

1 Thus *The Times* the weekend before we set off.

2 Carlo Giuliani was a twenty-three-year-old Italian anarchist shot dead by police, who then reversed a van over his body, during the Genoa protests. The film *Carlo Giuliani, Boy* (2002, general release) details his killing.

3 To get a sense of the kind of politics in which Corbyn was formed see Tony Benn's essays, *Arguments for Socialism* (Harmondsworth: Penguin, 1980). Political writing dates rapidly at the moment, but Richard Seymour's book is still a useful guide: *Corbyn: The Strange Rebirth of Radical Politics*, 2nd edition (London: Verso, 2017).

4 I thought about writing "creeds" here, but that is misleading. Both Christianity and Marxism are before anything else *practices*, ways of existing in the world. Christianity is first and foremost the collective practice of responding to what Christians take to be God's act of self-communication in Christ. Marxism is first and foremost the practice of criticizing society in concert with the struggle for working-class self-emancipation. Both *involve* believing certain propositions, and it is with this cognitive side of things that I will mainly be concerned here, but both are so much more.

[5]   Arun Kundnani, *The Muslims are Coming! Islamophobia, Extremism and the Domestic War on Terror* (London: Verso, 2015).

[6]   I'm leaving the north of Ireland out of consideration here, except by way of the influence of the DUP. The best accessible account of the manipulation of religious divisions in Ireland in the service of British rule remains the early parts of Eamonn McCann, *War and an Irish Town*, 3rd edition (Chicago, IL: Haymarket, 2018).

[7]   Grouped around the hard-right-wing fundamentalist Stephen Green, this group gives the impression of not having many members other than Green. Its website <https://www.christianvoice.org.uk/> is often unintentionally hilarious to those not signed up to its brand of stern biblicism. When I checked it on 20 February 2019, I learned that there had been "open-air prayer in West Ham", no doubt an event of great theologico-political importance, and I was told that the "Sussex Chief Constable had dishonoured his uniform at Gay Pride". This last story was a good deal less interesting than the strapline might suggest.

[8]   Andrew Collier, *Christianity and Marxism: A Philosophical Contribution to their Reconciliation* (London: Taylor & Francis, 2001).

[9]   Pelagianism being the view, regarded as heretical, that humanity can be redeemed (in the sense in which Christians mean that word) without Christ.

[10] The University of Hull, announcing the closure of philosophy programmes in late 2018, cited directly the needs of "business partners". See <http://dailynous.com/2018/12/19/

philosophy-hull-threatened-heads-39-uk-philosophy-departments-object/>. Thankfully the subsequent outcry won a reprieve, a valuable lesson in fighting back.

11 Karl Marx (1843), *A Contribution to the Critique of Hegel's Philosophy of Right: Introduction.* Available at <https://www.marxists.org/archive/marx/works/1843/critique-hpr/intro.html>.

12 On this see Denys Turner, "Marxism, Liberation and the Way of Negation", in Christopher Rowland (ed.), *The Cambridge Companion to Liberation Theology* (Cambridge: Cambridge University Press, 2007), pp. 229–47; and Alistair Kee, *Marx and the Failure of Liberation Theology* (London: SCM Press, 1990). The debate about the use of Marxist tools by Christian theologians has been most intense around Latin American liberation theology. A handy guide is Rosino Gibellini, *The Liberation Theology Debate* (London: SCM Press, 1987).

13 The focus on belief might seem surprising. In contemporary philosophy of religion there has been a movement against an excessive focus on belief at the expense of practice, often allied to political concerns. See e.g. Scrutton and Hewitt, "Philosophy of Living Religion: an Introduction", *International Journal of Philosophy and Theology* 79:4 (2018), pp. 349–54. Marx, however, differs from the mainstream of contemporary philosophy of religion in taking seriously the nature of belief as a socially situated phenomenon. Religious belief arises in definite social circumstances, and it is the relationship between the two which provides the material for his critique.

14 Marx (1843), *Contribution.*

15   Ludwig Feuerbach (1841), *The Essence of Christianity*. Available at <https://www.marxists.org/reference/archive/feuerbach/works/essence/>.

16   Karl Marx (1844), "On Alienated Labour", *Economic and Philosophical Manuscripts*.

17   "[I]t has to be noted that everything which appears in the worker as an *activity of alienation, of estrangement*, appears in the non-worker as a *state of alienation, of estrangement*", Marx (1844).

18   Of course, the fight against class society might, in particular circumstances, require attacks on particular forms of religious consciousness (and no Christian socialist should think otherwise!), but that is a matter of tactics rather than of first principles.

19   The New Atheists are usually thought to include at least Richard Dawkins, Christopher Hitchens, Daniel Dennett and Sam Harris.

20   *Philosophical Investigations*. Translated by G. E. M. Anscombe, P. M. S. Hacker, and Joachim Schulte, 4th edition (Oxford: Wiley Blackwell, 2009), p. 255.

21   See the essays in Mikel Burley (ed.), *Wittgenstein, Religion, and Ethics: New Perspectives from Philosophy and Theology* (London: Bloomsbury, 2018).

22   Well, that's not quite true: there is one (curious, and very bad) argument for atheism in the 1844 *Manuscripts*. See Allen W. Wood, *Karl Marx*, 2nd edition (London: Routledge, 2004), pp. 170 ff. for details.

23   What does 'have for' mean here? It depends if you are looking at things from the perspective of the atheist or the theist. Roughly things are as follows (no doubt finessing is needed to catch

stray cases.) For the Feuerbachian atheist, I can say something truthfully of God only if I deny that same thing of humanity. For the "Feuerbachian" theist, for all *F* in a significant class, God is *F* only if no human being is *F*. The reason that the two versions of the dilemma are phrased in significantly different ways is, of course, that the theist believes that God exists, whereas the atheist doesn't.

24 Karl Marx (1844), "Private Property and Communism", *Manuscripts*.

25 The key figure is Aquinas. Turner has written an excellent introduction: *Thomas Aquinas: A Portrait* (New Haven: Yale University Press, 2013). Aquinas' most important work, the *Summa Theologiae* (STh), is available at <http://www.newadvent.org/summa/>.

26 Denys Turner, "Feuerbach, Marx and reductivism", in Brian Davies (ed.), *Language, Meaning and God: Essays in Honour of Herbert McCabe OP* (London: Geoffrey Chapman, 1987), p. 103.

27 In Aquinas the path to this conclusion is via the doctrine of divine simplicity. See STh Ia, q3 and for an introduction Brian Davies, "A Modern Defence of Divine Simplicity", in *Philosophy of Religion: A Guide and Anthology* (Oxford: Oxford University Press, 2000), Ch. 52. I discuss the implications of this at book length in *Only the Splendour of Light: Apophatic Theology and Philosophy* (Leiden: Brill, forthcoming).

28 Herbert McCabe OP, *God Matters* (London: Geoffrey Chapman, 1987), p. 41. I have discussed the issues tackled in this section in greater detail in "Grammatical Thomism", *Religious Studies* (2019), <https://doi.org/10.1017/S0034412518000896>.

29   It's important to understanding this to realize that, contrary
      to creationism (and the early modern deism with which its
      proponents would be horrified to discover it has much in
      common), Creation, as God's act of giving being to the world,
      is not simply a matter of God winding up the world at the
      beginning and letting it run. It is logically possible, after all,
      that the world has no beginning. Rather creation is a matter of
      everything other than God depending on God for its existence at
      every moment it exists. God's agency is therefore of a completely
      different order from that of a created cause.

30   For the sake of Marxism geeks: by "transcended", I mean
      "*aufgehoben*".

31   In the context of debates around non-theistic authors such as
      Don Cupitt and Anthony Freeman it is commonplace in some
      circles to make belief in "an interventionist God" the touchstone
      of orthodoxy. Much though I disagree with Cupitt and Freeman
      (and the bourgeois conformism they represent), this way of
      stating matters is itself stuck in the Feuerbachian problematic.
      One can only intervene from outside a situation. Now, I am
      outside Leeds, and the Earth is outside the Orion nebula, but
      God is not outside anywhere. God does not have spatial location
      yet is immediately present to everything as its Creator.

32   By the "Hebrew Bible" I mean the *tanach* or canonical Jewish
      scriptures, which are co-extensive with the Old Testament
      of Protestant Christianity. Although the phrase is often used
      synonymously with "Old Testament" in academic and other
      circles, this is misleading—Catholics accept the so-called
      deuterocanonical books, present in the Greek version of the
      Old Testament, and members of Orthodox churches even more.

Since I'm referring to a theological theme prominent in the Hebrew books here, the distinction doesn't matter.

33 The original fills out the Hebrew name of God, which is not spoken in routine Jewish practice. I've replaced it with "the Lord" in accordance with current Catholic practice. Both are gestures towards the radical mystery of God, so appropriate for the present subject matter.

34 McCabe, "The Involvement of God", in *God Matters*, p. 43.

35 See further McCabe's essay "Freedom", in *God Matters*, pp. 10–24.

36 The full text is available at <http://www.trotsky.net/trotsky_year/political_testament.html>.

37 For contemporary philosophical treatments of pantheism and other "non-classical" conceptions of deity see Andrei Buckareff and Yujin Nagasawa (eds), *Alternative Concepts of God* (Oxford: Oxford University Press, 2016).

38 See Terry Eagleton, *Why Marx Was Right* (New Haven: Yale University Press, 2011), pp. 128–29.

39 The anti-metaphysical critic is, "a brother metaphysician with a rival theory of first principles". F. H. Bradley, *Appearance and Reality* (London: George Allen and Unwin, 1893), p. 1.

40 David Harvey draws attention to this when writing about *Capital*: *A Companion to Marx's Capital: Volume 1* (London: Verso, 2010), p. 33.

41 A good example is Brian Epstein, *The Ant Trap: Rebuilding the Foundations of the Social Sciences* (Oxford: Oxford University Press, 2015).

42 See Michèle Friend, *Introducing Philosophy of Mathematics* (Stocksfield: Acumen, 2007).

[43]   Karl Marx, *Theses on Feuerbach* (1845), 11. Available at <https://www.marxists.org/archive/marx/works/1845/theses/index.htm>.

[44]   *The Eighteenth Brumaire of Louis Bonaparte* (1852), Ch. 1. Available at <https://www.marxists.org/archive/marx/works/1852/18th-brumaire/ch01.htm>. I've modified the translation to avoid using "men" for generic humanity.

[45]   It is important, I think, to be clear that Marx is concerned with social *explanation*. Although it wouldn't be to Marx's taste, I do not think there is anything in historical materialism that rules out a place for myths, or for theological stories about human history. Ideological obfuscation arises when we mistake these things for competitors for social scientific explanation.

[46]   Both "production" and "needs" have broad readings in Marx. Production is any activity that gives rise to what he calls a use-value, something with the capacity to satisfy human needs or desire. In this sense, an actor performing a play or a person in an electricity company's call centre are producing (there is a more technical sense of "productive" in Marx's economic writings; we needn't concern ourselves with that here). Human needs are historically changing and arise not only from our biology but from our social nature. It is not absurd to say that I need a mobile phone, and all of us need leisure activities.

[47]   For a much more detailed overview see Chapter 2 of G. A. Cohen, *Karl Marx's Theory of History: A Defence* (Oxford: Oxford University Press, 1979).

[48]   Of course, in slave-owning societies ownership has extended over human beings.

[49]   For present purposes, wages include what we would call *salaries*.

50 Karl Marx (1859), *A Contribution to the Critique of Political Economy: Preface*. Available at <https://www.marxists.org/archive/marx/works/1859/critique-pol-economy/preface.htm>.

51 Karl Marx and Friedrich Engels, "Ruling Class and Ruling Ideas", *German Ideology*.

52 Karl Marx and Friedrich Engels, *German Ideology*.

53 Plato, *Meno*. Available at <http://classics.mit.edu/Plato/meno.html>.

54 A target, not *the* target: especially in the *Theses on Feuerbach*. Marx also has crude forms of materialism in mind, those with a mechanically reductive view of human beings, ignoring both our social nature and our capacities to consciously engage with the world intellectually and transform it by deliberate action.

55 George Berkeley, *A Treatise Concerning the Principles of Human Knowledge* (1734). Available at <https://www.maths.tcd.ie/~dwilkins/Berkeley/HumanKnowledge/1734/HumKno.pdf>.

56 G. W. F. Hegel, *Phenomenology of Spirit* (1807). Available at <https://www.marxists.org/reference/archive/hegel/phindex.htm>. Note that this version translates the German *Geist* as "Mind" in the title.

57 Lenin remarked: "It is impossible completely to understand Marx's *Capital*, and especially its first chapter, without having thoroughly studied and understood the whole of Hegel's *Logic*. Consequently, half a century later none of the Marxists understood Marx!" (*Collected Works*, Vol. 38, p. 180). Since I think the world would be much better off if more people understood Marx, I hope that Lenin was wrong!

58 Marx and Engels, *German Ideology*.

59   Classics include Sheila Rowbotham, Lynne Segal, and Hilary Wainwright, *Beyond the Fragments: Feminism and the Making of Socialism* (London: Merlin Press, 1979); Michelle Barrett, *Women's Oppression Today: The Marxist/Feminist Encounter*, New edition (London: Verso, 2014). A useful Marxist–feminist approach to contemporary questions is Nina Power, *One Dimensional Woman* (London: Zero, 2009).

60   I'm indebted for this soundbite to the title of Lorna Finlayson's excellent *The Political is Political: Conformity and the Illusion of Dissent in Contemporary Political Philosophy* (London: Rowan and Littlefield, 2015).

61   A minor curiosity that could be mentioned here is the presence in academia of a Christian idealism focused on intellectual history, Radical Orthodoxy. See my review of Adrian Pabst, "Metaphysics: The Creation of Hierarchy", *Journal of Theological Studies* 67:1 (2016), pp. 399–403.

62   See Alistair Kee, *Marx and the Failure of Liberation Theology* (London: SCM Press, 1990), p. 212. Kee discusses Boff's *Church, Charism and Power: Liberation Theology and the Institutional Church* (London: SCM Press, 1985).

63   The Congregation for the Doctrine of the Faith's 1984 *Instruction on certain elements of the 'theology of liberation'* is available at <http://www.vatican.va/roman_curia/congregations/cfaith/documents/rc_con_cfaith_doc_19840806_theology-liberation_en.html>.

64   Avery Dulles, *Models of the Church*, 2nd edition (Harmondsworth: Bantam, 1991).

65   Compare Vološinov, "Any ideological product is not only itself a part of reality . . . [it also] reflects and refracts another reality outside itself. Everything ideological possesses *meaning*: it

represents, depicts, or stands for something lying outside itself. In other words it is a *sign. Without signs there is no ideology",* *Marxism and the Philosophy of Language.* Russian original 1929. Translated by Ladislav Matejka and I. R. Titunik (Cambridge, MA: Harvard University Press, 1986), p. 9.

66 Modern ears are likely to hear "all things but sin" as a pretty big exception, since we are prone to think of sin as essential to human beings (witness the way we respond to pious injunctions to reform our behaviour by appealing to "human nature"). To understand what Chalcedon is getting at here we need to look at sin at a lack, a failure to be human, such that if someone is without sin, they are more human in virtue of that. From this perspective, those of us who sin are less human than we could be. As we'll see later on Marx agrees that this is the lot of most human beings.

67 Dulles, *Models of the Church.*

68 In this section I'm drawing on ideas I first heard from the Anglican socialist theologian Ken Leech and the tradition he represents. See for example *The Sky is Red: Discerning the Signs of the Times,* new edition (London: Darton, Longman and Todd, 2003).

69 Marx, *Theses on Feuerbach.*

70 Gilbert Ryle notes the religious motivation for mind-body dualism in his classic *The Concept of Mind* (Chicago: University of Chicago Press, 2002). Originally published 1949.

71 Luke 1:53.

72 The New Testament *pneumatikou,* rendered "spiritual", can mean "of the Spirit". On this reading for something to be spiritual is not for it to be non-material but for it to somehow

pertain to the work of the Holy Spirit. Feeding the poor can be spiritual in this sense, for example.

73   Genesis 1.

74   "*Anima mea non est ego*", *Super primum epistolam ad corinthios*, 1:10.

75   Karl Marx and Friedrich Engels, *The Communist Manifesto*. Available at <https://www.marxists.org/archive/marx/works/download/pdf/Manifesto.pdf>, p. 20.

76   Marx and Engels, *Manifesto*, p. 34. I have altered the Moore translation to avoid the unwarranted masculine "working men". The German is "*Proletarier*".

77   Marx and Engels, *Manifesto.*

78   Vladimir Lenin, *State and Revolution*, <https://www.marxists.org/archive/lenin/works/1917/staterev/ch01.htm#s2>. Ch. 2, "Special Bodies of Armed Men, Prisons etc.".

79   James Connolly, *Labour, Nationality and Religion*, <https://www.marxists.org/archive/connolly/1910/lnr/index.htm>.

80   Herbert McCabe, "The Class Struggle and Christian Love", in *God Matters*, pp. 182–98. I have discussed the topic of this section in "On Not Crying 'Peace'—The Theological Politics of Herbert McCabe", *New Blackfriars* 99: 1084 (2018), pp. 740–55.

81   McCabe, *Class Struggle*, p. 188.

82   McCabe, *Class Struggle*, p. 190.

83   McCabe, *Class Struggle*, p. 185.

84   I have in mind the Roman Rite mass here. In Anglican practice (and other liturgies, such as the Ambrosian), the sign of peace occurs earlier in the liturgy.

85   There has been a fashion for substituting "reign" for "kingdom" recently as a translation of the New Testament Greek *basileia*.

Often motivated by political sensibility the preference seems to me to trade on the dubious idea that reigns are better than kingdoms. In any case, either way, talk of God's kingdom/ reign is only acceptable if we frankly admit that it is a parody of human systems of domination, in which the hungry are fed, and God alone rules (which is, of course, to say that no being is ruler over another).

[86]   Revelation 21:1; Romans 8.

[87]   The synoptic Gospels—Matthew, Mark and Luke—are so-called because they narrate the life and ministry of Jesus with a similar "shape", as though seen with the same eye. The dominant position in biblical studies (with which I agree) has it that this is because Mark wrote first and Matthew and Luke subsequently, with access to Mark and adopting his narrative as a skeleton for their own. On Jesus and the Kingdom see, for instance, Edward Schillebeeckx, *Church: The Human Story of God* (London: SCM Press, 1989), Ch. 3, sec. 2.

[88]   "Charity" in non-religious English conjures up images of raffles and foodbanks. The Latin *caritas* suggests, by contrast, something like a radical form of friendship.

[89]   Of course, even that needn't be merely a sign. Imagine that I wrote it in chalk on the road leading up to an RAF bomber base! Still, in speaking of a sign as a sacrament, I am saying some very particular things. For Catholic theology, I am saying that, by virtue of God's guarantee and gift of the Holy Spirit, the sign can never fail to make present that which it signifies (however opaque the symbolism may be made by human sinfulness)— the eucharist is still the Body of Christ, even though it be

consecrated and distributed by a high-and-mighty priest with a class-divided congregation.

90   Revelation 5:9.

91   Marx and Engels, *Manifesto*, p. 1.

92   I acknowledge my debt here to the pulpit scene from Ken Loach's *The Wind That Shakes the Barley*.

93   Rosa Luxemburg, *Socialism and the Churches*. Available at <https://www.marxistsfr.org/archive/luxemburg/1905/misc/socialism-churches.htm>.

94   William Blake, *The Complete Poems*. Edited by Alicia Ostriker. (Harmondsworth: Penguin, 1977).

95   William Blake, *The Marriage of Heaven and Hell*. Edited by Geoffrey Keynes. (Oxford: Oxford University Press, 1975).

96   Aristotle, *Nicomachean Ethics*. Available at <http://classics.mit.edu/Aristotle/nicomachaen.html>.

97   The foundational text is usually thought to be G. E. M. Anscombe, "Modern Moral Philosophy", *Philosophy* 33 (1958). Prominent thinkers associated with the tradition include, as well as Anscombe, Philippa Foot and Alisdair MacIntyre. On the relationship between Marxism and virtue ethics see Paul Blackledge, *Marxism and Ethics: Freedom, Desire and Revolution* (New York: SUNY Press, 2013).

98   In actual fact one doesn't need to be a celebrity to be subject to censure by popular moralism. In 2013, when setting off from Heathrow to South Africa, Justine Sacco tweeted "Going to Africa. Hope I don't get AIDS. Just kidding. I'm white!" Over the course of her eleven-hour flight, the hashtag #HasJustineLandedYet trended, and large amounts of abuse were tweeted at the PR executive, who was sacked from her

job for the tweet. See "How One Stupid Tweet Blew up Justine Sacco's Life", *New York Times*, 12 February 2015. Her intention was to mock racism, but more interesting than the ethics of her tweet is the moralism of the Twitter mob.

[99] The most prominent far-right critic of campus life is currently Jordan Peterson, whose work I will not gratify with a reference. That someone like Peterson has acquired something like celebrity status shows, I think, why the left itself ought to have an autonomous critique of liberal moralism. Failure in this respect leaves people disquieted with the alienated and alienating *status quo* with the far right as the only oppositional option.

[100] I'm drawing here on ideas concerning 'internal reasons', which Bernard Williams develops in *Moral Luck* (Cambridge: Cambridge University Press, 1981).

[101] As Wittgenstein would put it, it is part of the grammar of "fulfilment" that we seek fulfilment.

[102] G. E. M. Anscombe, "Modern Moral Philosophy", *Philosophy* 33 (1958), pp. 1–19.

[103] G. E. M. Anscombe, *Intention* (Oxford: Basil Blackwell, 1957).

[104] Aristotle, *Nicomachean Ethics* I.2.

[105] See Paul Blackledge, *Marxism and Ethics: Freedom, Desire and Revolution* (New York: SUNY Press, 2012).

[106] Rooted in Marx's work, the canonical distinction between scientific and utopian socialism is in Engels' 1880 *Socialism: Utopian and Scientific*, <https://www.marxists.org/archive/marx/works/1880/soc-utop/index.htm>.

[107] Under the influence of Louis Althusser, some have exaggerated the distance between Marx's early and late works. The classic exposition of a view which sees alienation as a unifying

theme through his work is Istvan Meszaros, *Marx's Theory of Alienation*, 5th edition (London: Merlin, 2005).

[108] It's worth noting though that the contemporary right (for a prominent example, see Jordan Peterson, mentioned above) systematically elides Marxism and postmodernism. Since on many points, human nature being one, Marxists and postmodernists adopt mutually contradictory positions, the left ought to be clear about the differences between the two. See Terry Eagleton, *The Illusions of Postmodernism* (Oxford: Blackwell, 1992).

[109] <https://www.marxists.org/archive/marx/works/1844/manuscripts/labour.htm>. Note the title on *Marxists* is "Estranged Labour"—I've used the alternative translation which fits better with the topic.

[110] A good book on Marx's account of human nature (and a defence of the view that he had such an account) is Norman Geras, *Marx and Human Nature: The Refutation of a Legend*, Radical Thinkers Series (London: Verso, 2016).

[111] <https://www.marxists.org/archive/marx/works/1867-c1/ch07.htm>.

[112] Karl Marx, *Estranged Labour.*

[113] It was William Morris who most obviously lived out this view of the human person in theory and in practice (interestingly he did not have access to the 1844 *Manuscripts*). See his *News from Nowhere and Other Writings* (Harmondsworth: Penguin, 1993).

[114] Theodor Adorno, *Minima moralia*, 18. <https://www.marxists.org/reference/archive/adorno/1951/mm/ch01.htm>.

[115] Mark 12:29–31.

116 STh IIi, q1, a7. (I've altered the Blackfriars translation to remove a superfluous "men"). Augustine, *De Trinitate*, xiii, 3.

117 If it ever really was the case that human beings were capable only of natural flourishing: a theme of much Catholic theology since the mid-twentieth century, and especially apparent in the work of Karl Rahner, is the universality of grace—at no point is any human being "merely" human, she is always already somehow subject to the offer of God's grace. For a good introduction see William Dych SJ, *Karl Rahner* (London: Continuum, 1992), Ch. 3.

118 This traditional list of the so-called theological virtues is taken from 1 Corinthians 13:13. There is much more that would be said in a longer account of the understanding of virtue in Christianity. In particular, Aquinas' account of *infused moral virtue*, according to which the life of grace feeds even "natural" human flourishing is both fascinating and important.

119 STh Ia, q1, a8, ad. 2.

120 See Peter Hebblethwaite, *Christian Marxist Dialogue* (London: Darton, Longman, and Todd, 1977).

121 Tony Benn, 'Revolutionary Christianity', *Marxism Today* (January 1980). Available at <https://jacobinmag.com/2018/12/tony-benn-christianity-socialism-neighborly-love>.

122 Revelation 21:22.

123 On fascism see Mark Neocleous, *Fascism* (Buckingham: Open University Press, 1997). His writing on fascism and death is salient here too: *The Monstrous and the Dead: Burke, Marx, Fascism* (Cardiff: University of Wales Press, 2005).

124 1 Peter 3:15.

125 Eagleton's *Hope Without Optimism* (New Haven: Yale University Press, 2015) is an important recent contribution on political hope.

[126] I hereby disown the silly phrase "post-industrial". The fact that a society is consuming electronic equipment made by workers on poverty wages on the other side of a globe no more makes it "post-industrial" than a male chauvinist is post-housework because his wife does the ironing.

[127] And these forms of reaction, which feed off social and cultural dislocation, are more than capable of wrapping themselves in religious garb. At the time of writing a couple of organizers for the neo-fascist youth group Generation Identity in Britain claim to be Catholic. Christianity is not simply a movement whose future is a matter of political contest; our present identity and allegiance are up for grabs.

Lightning Source UK Ltd.
Milton Keynes UK
UKHW020639060820
367798UK00012B/1210